HAS AFRICA SHED

ITS

"THIRD WORLD" STATUS?

and other thought-provoking essays

Peter de Haan

HAS AFRICA SHED

ITS

"THIRD WORLD" STATUS?

and other thought-provoking essays

Peter de Haan

The Lembani Trust
Lusaka

http://sites.google.com/site/lembanitrust/

First published 2010 by the Lembani Trust
Lusaka, Zambia

Printed by Printech Ltd., 211 229590

ISBN 978-9982-9972-9-4

Table of Contents

Introduction

This book contains a collection of articles which I published in *The Post Newspaper* between November 2007 and July 2010. Why, for heaven's sake, would one write articles in a newspaper? That's a good question which deserves an honest answer. In my case, there is no one answer to this probing question; there are more than one. Let me start with the beginning, which concerned a review of Paul Collier's book: *The Bottom Billion* which came out in 2007. The year before I had published a book on development and I had promised myself not to write for a long time. Collier's book drew quite some attention; I read it and thought to myself, why don't I write a brief review and ask my boss whether I'd be allowed to publish it? I had to ask permission because during that time I was working at the Netherlands Embassy in Lusaka. My ambassador graciously granted permission. My Zambian colleague at the time, Judith Kumwenda, knew an editor at *The Post*, and to my delight, the paper published it, and continued to publish all the others I wrote.

Writing is addictive; once I had started again I couldn't stop. And I really enjoyed it. The enjoyment not only came from studying contemporary and historical-development issues, but also from moulding them in a readable manner and that is what I have tried to do. Another mighty inspiration was the fan mail I got! Increasingly the mail came from students. That was very inspirational as these students will in future very probably help design and implement Zambia's development. It is for them in particular that I decided to collect my writings in this booklet. My publisher, the Lembani Trust, accepted the manuscript and the result you hold in your hands.

Obviously, this book is not only the result of my efforts. Invaluable and often constructive criticism I received from: Herman Abels, Mercy Banda, Maarten Brouwer, Alex Chileshe, Robert van den Dool, Alfonso Garcia, Bruno Giussani, André Loozekoot, Eddy Middeldorp, Harry Molenaar, Patricia Palale, David Roodman, Marein van Schaaijk, and Rene Smulders.

Esineya Sakala Phiri assisted me greatly with typing some parts of the manuscript and with its lay-out.

My wife, Dr. Marisales Ramon-Chorda, did review all the articles from their first draft to the final product. She is a woman of few words. When I asked her: What do you think of this piece? and she would say: 'Hm', I knew that it was not good enough. However, when she responded: 'Good', then I knew it was publishable. I thank her, with great affection, for her unwavering support.

Lusaka
October, 2010

AFRICA, ASIA &
LATIN AMERICA

Has Africa Shed its "Third World" Status?

'It was the best of times; it was the worst of times', that is how Charles Dickens' *A tale of Two Cities* begins. I was reminded of this brilliant phrase when reading the British weekly newspaper *The Economist* the other day. It was running a special report on South Africa which was not particularly uplifting, so to speak. But columnist *Schumpeter* dealt with Africa's positive aspects--a far more inspiring piece of writing! I was puzzled, as my perception of Africa's future was not very positive! And if that was not all, the newspaper also ran an article inspired by World Bank President Bob Zoellick's observation that: '2009 saw the end of what was known as the third world'. So, did I have to change my perception about Africa and the third world at large?

Let me first share with you the good news about Africa. Schumpeter's column noted that the 21st century is the century of the emerging economies, just as the 20th century was America's century and the 19th century was that of Britain. The question is: which economies will be emerging? Already a few have qualified such as Brazil, Russia, India and China; the so-called BRIC group. With the exception of Botswana and South Africa, I believe that none of the other African countries would stand a chance to qualify, or am I wrong?

Schumpeter offers a few arguments which could unleash the African lion; like the Chinese dragon and the Indian tiger before. In the period 2000-2008 Africa's annual output grew by almost 5 %, which is twice as fast as during the two preceding decades. I believe that the best way to get out of poverty is through sustained economic growth. But can Africa get that done despite three major hindering factors? They are: dysfunctional politics, Africa's dependency on the exploitation of natural resources, and number three is that Africa's growth doesn't trickle down to the poor. However, are these factors still valid? Not exactly, says Schumpeter. There are glimmers of hope! Inflation has been brought down from 22 % in the 1990s to an average of 8 % since 2000. Rwanda is the top-performer according to the World Bank's latest *Doing Business* report, which measures the promotion of entrepreneurship. As for natural resources' contribution to growth, this

2

sector contributes not more than a third of the continent's growth. There are other industries, besides mining, which contribute to Africa's growth. Take SABMiller, the South African brewer, which is the world's second largest. Aspen Pharmacare of South Africa is the largest generic-drug maker in the southern hemisphere. Mention must also be made of Tunisia's Coficab, one of the world's largest suppliers of wiring for cars. And who hasn't heard of billionaire-philanthropist Mo Ibrahim, who created Celtel?

As for *the bottom billion,* that is the poor, thanks to the gradual rise in living standards, it is expected that some 200 million Africans will enter the market for consumer goods soon. Looking at the expansion of Lusaka's Manda Hill Shopping Centre and the vigorous growth of some of Zambia's smaller cities, I must admit that Zambia's purchasing power is indeed growing! If further growth would keep pace with Africa's rapidly growing population (from 500 million now to an estimated 1.2 billion in 2040), that would attract the attention of giant consumer goods multinationals such as Unilever and Procter & Gamble, as well as Chinese and Indian automakers.

There is also innovation! Take mobile phones. They have already given a lot of poor farmers information on what their produce can fetch on the market. E-banking is another aspect which will ease money transfers and the quick supply of credit. These are just a few *bottom of the pyramid* innovations. Others include the Jiko, a portable charcoal stove that reduces fuel consumption; the Q-drum, a doughnut-shaped plastic container that can be used to transport water by rolling it along the ground, and the Weza, a foot-powered generator that can be used to charge cell phones and radios. By the way, the expression *bottom of the pyramid* is a reference to C.K. Prahalad's book *The Fortune at the Bottom of the Pyramid,* wherein a passionate plea for the poor as economic actors is made; they form a formidable group of consumers.

Let's now look at South Africa. The country was near bankrupt when apartheid ended. Now it is a middle-income developing country with a GDP per person of around $10,000 at purchasing power parity. This average doesn't reflect the wide income distribution: almost half the population lives below the poverty line of $2 per day. The whites have by and large done better than most blacks since apartheid ended. It is true that the poor now receive more government support than in the old days; yet, most of them live in crime-ridden shanty towns where schools and clinics are in a dire state.

What is happening in South Africa reminds me of what was happening in Germany after the unification in 1989 between (rich) West Germany and impoverished East Germany. Billions of Euros were pumped into East Germany, and there still is a large divide in terms of employment and wealth between the Western and Eastern part of the country. In other words, it takes a lot of time, money, and patience to straighten things out. The challenge for the South African government is that the poor black population expects improvements sooner and that creates tensions. As the great French political philosopher de Tocqueville wisely noted: 'Revolutions tend to start with rising expectations, not when conditions are at their worst'.

South Africa's growth is insufficient to bring down the very high unemployment rate (25 %). It doesn't keep up in competitiveness with other emerging countries such as China and India. This also applies to higher education. The non-white vice-chancellor of the University of the Free State lamented that the country has no 'great' universities; it has only a few good ones. The University of Cape Town is the only African university to be ranked among the world's top 200. Compare this with what the Chinese are doing. China recognizes the importance of an educated work force for economic growth; moreover, investing in research makes its economy more innovative and competitive. China wants to create a few world-class universities (in some cases in cooperation with American top universities). China is investing heavily to double the number of institutions of higher learning. Government's investment in research and development also more than doubled over the past decade. Even though South Africa would be the potential African candidate to join the BRIC group, it is already falling behind the likes of China and India in competitiveness and investing into its future generations.

Given all this, what did Bob Zoellick mean when he said that the third world ended in 2009? Surely, he wasn't blind to the fact that the poorest of the poor live in-precisely- third world countries. The world is still divided in

4

the haves and have-nots. What he meant is that the *composition* of the third world has altered. In the old days the third world was associated with economic failures, running irresponsible fiscal and monetary policies and with aid dependency.

That has definitely changed. Yet, some 60 countries (unfortunately most African) retain third world characteristics; home to 1 billion poor people, aid dependent, here and there violent, and sometimes corrupt. On the other hand, quite a few former poor-but now emerging-economies ended donor support and even register far higher growth rates than developed countries. The latter ones are now in financial trouble. They are the ones to depend on IMF bail-outs, whilst the emerging ones don't need that kind of support. Since 2008 the emerging economies contributed almost all of the world's economic growth, says the World Bank. They are becoming the engines of the world economy. They invest in US government bonds and in foreign capital investment. China finances oil refineries in Nigeria worth more than $23 billion, which is nearly twice the total increase in aid to Africa over the past 5 years. This triggered a former Nigerian finance minister to say that: 'It was high time that Africa saw and presented itself as the fifth BRIC, an attractive destination for investment, and not just aid'.

Another aspect is that developing countries, such as Zambia, have weathered the financial crisis much better than rich countries. They keep on growing, while Europe, Japan, and the USA struggle to pull their economies out of the slump. Their public debt is rising above 100 % of GDP, while debt of emerging markets is dropping to 40 % of GDP.

Re-designing the world's economic map is justified and overdue. When taking a look at this new map, the emerging economies have visibly putting themselves on that map. But, what about Africa? When I saw such a map the other day, Africa is depicted as a small appendix, hanging underneath the fat bellies of China, India and Europe; so, graphically refuting the statement that the third world has ended. I fear that if Africa doesn't take up the challenge posed by the emerging economies, it will be ever more difficult to become an 'emerging' continent.

(2010)

Growth and Poverty in Zambia

Zambia has seen bouts of economic growth since independence from Britain on October 24, 1964. Zambia also receives foreign investment and a lot of foreign aid. The question is: did growth, investment and aid help reduce poverty?

I believe that without economic growth poverty cannot be reduced. After all, equally distributing a small economic 'cake' amongst a large group of people would make everybody equally poor. We need a bigger cake to overcome poverty. Of course, other aspects also play a role such as health and education accessible to all, a just tax system, and a well functioning public sector. A country's infrastructure should also be in order. The investment climate should be favourable, the Rule of Law should be upheld and corruption should be held in check.

Very important is sound economic policies. Look at the Asian countries which managed to grow spectacularly after World War II. This was triggered by sound economic policies of their governments. In economics this is more and more recognized as an important explanatory element and it is captured under the term *political economy*. Politics and economics can be a successful combination. Unfortunately, in quite a few African countries it isn't. I would describe political economics in those cases as *economic commonsense diluted by political considerations*.

Being poor is awful. One stands to lose one's dignity; poor parents can't send their children to school; and, what happens when a family member falls ill or dies? Poverty may also trigger instability. It is for these reasons that combating poverty is an important social, economic, political (and I would even say moral) objective of any responsible government. Government leaders the world over agreed at the UN in New York in 2000 that they would bring absolute poverty down by half in 2015.

Zambia has its poverty reduction program, and the donors are here mainly to help Zambia to fight poverty. However, Zambia was poor and still is: 64 % of all Zambians are poor. A lot of studies have been undertaken in

Zambia to find out where exactly the poor live, how they cope and -very importantly- whether the gap between rich and poor widened or not. These poverty studies are often more sophisticated than only measuring income. As many poor Zambians hardly take part in the formal monetized economy, it is not so much their income that counts; it is other things such as access to health and education which better measures poverty.

Now, what do these studies tell us? A recent study of the University of Cape Town concludes that over the period 1996 - 2006, poverty in Zambia did not change much, with the exception of the urban poor; they did a bit better. Poverty remains a predominantly rural phenomenon; some rural poor even got poorer. Poverty rates are highest amongst small and medium-sized farmers and non-farm rural residents. When looking at poverty with a gender perspective, the study concluded that female-headed households are disproportionally poor in Zambia.

What about the interaction between economic growth and poverty? It was reported that economic growth did take place between 1996 and 2006. The growth rate varied between 3 and 6 percent per year. This decade long consistent economic growth benefitted, as already noted, the urban population but it didn't 'trickle down' to the rural poor.

Despite this recent growth period Zambia's per capita income is still below the per capita income at independence. Zambia's stagnant development is difficult to understand given its rich copper deposits and its abundant potential in agriculture, energy and tourism.

What went wrong, what counter-productive policies were adopted and where did the donors contributions go to? Newly independent Zambia started well in that the government opted for a market economy. Mining and urban areas were favoured through import substitution financed by the growing copper income. Foreign investment in mining rose rapidly, and so did Gross Domestic Product. But only few people benefitted; particularly the rural areas were left out. Accordingly, inequality which was already high prior to independence worsened.

After the collapse of the copper prices in the early 1970's, government opted for *state control* of the economy. And from that time onwards things did not fare well. Falling copper income forced the Government to borrow heavily; foreign debt rose while GDP growth dropped to an average of 0.5%. Rather than initiating a process of structural adjustment (that would have been a common sense decision) to put order in government's finances, it chose to adopt control mechanisms such as subsidizing urban consumption. The mining sector and state-owned manufacturing firms were favoured through import licensing and foreign exchange allocations, to the detriment of social spending and investment in rural infrastructure.

By the end of the 1970's government admitted that its economic policies were wrong and started to implement its first structural adjustment program (SAP). However, political will to implement it was half hearted, so that by the middle of the 1980's subsidies again comprised a sizeable chunk of the fiscal budget, while price controls made many state enterprises unprofitable. Inflation was over 180 % in the early 1990's.

One success of the SAP was the regaining of macro-economic stability, including bringing the inflation rate below 10 %. Loss- making state-run companies were sold. The SAP also included civil service reform (CSR). This was an important aspect as Government's wage bill was more than 40 % of the budget. The key word in CSR was *downsizing*. Fifteen thousand civil servants were sacked initially. However, later on the number of civil servants rose again to the original levels. Civil service pay rose, at the detriment of spending in health, education and other social services, which could have contributed to the fight against poverty. Moreover, the present salary and incentive structure does not promote better service delivery: the basic salaries are too low across the board. This induces civil servants to augment their income through generous sitting and travel allowances provided when attending seminars and courses, which take them away from their core tasks, such as attending to patients or instructing pupils.

Past agricultural policies also did not help much. They limited diversification. Maize growing was promoted through production and fertilizer subsidies, to the extent that it shifted production away from more competitive products. Accordingly, agriculture's export potential was undermined and farmers grew maize in areas that were not always best suited to this drought susceptible crop. The good news is that Zambia's agricultural sector is catching up. More agricultural produce is being exported and the share of agriculture in Zambia's total export hovers around 20 %.

Taking the period 1980 - 2002 into consideration, Zambia's average per capita growth was -1.8 %, while it received the highest ratio of aid/GDP of almost all African countries. This inverse relation reminds me of a critic of the Soviet Union who was asked what the reason for its collapse was. He jokingly explained it by saying that every night enormous truckloads of goods were transported to Siberia where these loads were dumped into a huge hole. What he-of course-meant is that when a country invests in unproductive goods and services, it undermines its long-term sustainability.

Poverty is best attacked by a mix of sustained economic growth and effective government service delivery. Zambia is expensive and its productivity is low triggered by poor infrastructure, limited energy and credit supply. All this limits job and income creation and further economic growth, which in turn hinders the fight against poverty. Government needs to see to it that the private sector can avail of better infrastructure, sufficient energy supply and better trained people; hence dramatic improvement in skills training and secondary and university education is a must, if Zambia wishes to make a real impact in the fight against poverty. The donors can help; perhaps they have to act more business-like, in that tangible results of donors' support to growth and poverty reduction would promote future growth and development.

(2009)

9

Do the Millennium Development Goals Make Sense for Africa?

In 2000 most world leaders gathered at the Millennium Summit in New York where they all committed to halving poverty by 2015. A person is absolutely poor if he or she lives of less than $1 a day. This objective raises three questions. First, why did the world leaders agree to this objective, which -incidentally- is the first of the eight Millennium Development Goals (MDGs) agreed upon in New York? Question number two is *how* the MDGs are measured? The third question is: can Africa achieve them?

The why question must be seen in the following context: The world of international cooperation has -over its half century existence- tried successive development philosophies, such as filling the financing gap, the big push, basic needs and -lately- good governance. None of them brought the sustained economic growth the donors were supposed to promote. Why this succession of models? Because new models provide fresh expectations that *this* time they will work. But time and again they didn't. Public opinion in the donor countries was favourable towards aid giving. But this is changing. Tax payers want to see results; their patience is running out. Moreover, stories about wasted money and corruption do not help to turn the tide. The present economic crisis puts aid under pressure, despite the fact that the poorest of the poor suffer most from it. Now, in order to show results, the MDGs provide the yardsticks. But do they, and are the MDGs fair to Africa?

Foreign aid critic, William Easterly, wrote a sharp analysis of the MDGs. His article *'How the Millennium Development Goals are unfair to Africa'*, denounces the typical observation that Africa will miss all the MDGs.

Let me first summarise what the MDGs are all about. MDG 1 is, as already explained, about halving the number of poor who live below the absolute poverty line by 2015. MDG 2 measures the attainment of 100 % primary school enrolment. MDG 3 deals with gender equality. As for health, there are a few MDGs. For example, MDG 4 is about reducing child mortality by two-thirds. MDG 5 aims to bring down maternal mortality, also by two-thirds. Regarding AIDS, TB and malaria, MDG 6 is to halt and

10

reverse the spread of these killer diseases. MDG 7 measures people without access to clean water. Finally, MDG 8 refers to donor harmonisation.

Easterly says about Africa's performance in achieving the MDG's that, although Africa performance is not good in all areas, its performance looks worse because of the particular way in which the MDG targets are set. As a result African successes are portrayed as failures! And that is strange, as the MDGs were -amongst others- launched to draw special attention to Africa. Easterly demonstrates that because of the wide variety in target setting, Africa's progress looks worse than is justified. Let me take you through Easterly's arguments.

Regarding MDG number one, halving absolute poverty by 2015, many development economists say that poverty is best reduced through robust economic growth. However, we know that the lower the per capita income, the higher the growth rate has to be to lift people out of poverty. Africa is disadvantaged in achieving MDG 1 by having the lowest per capita income of any region in the world. Africa's growth record in the period 2000 - 2007 was vey commendable, registering an average GDP growth of 5.2 %. Even if Africa were continue to grow at 5.2 %, still it wouldn't be able to reach MDG 1, because the number of poor and their very low levels of income would require Africa to grow at least at 7 % per annum over the next decade. So, the bias against Africa in the first MDG comes from penalizing it for its high initial poverty rate.

Now let us look at MDG 2: the attainment of universal primary education by 2015. This goal is formulated in end-goal terms. This creates an obvious bias against Africa, which started off farthest from the absolute target of 100 %. Researcher Michael Clemens says that most African countries have actually expanded primary school enrolments far more rapidly over the past 50 years than Western countries did during their development, but still Africans would not reach the target of universal enrolment by 2015. The World Bank condemned Burkina Faso in 2003 as seriously `off track` to meet MDG 2, yet, the country has expanded elementary education at more than twice the rate of Western historical experience! There is more to be said about this MDG. First, would it not have made much more sense to measure primary school *completion* rather than enrolment? Second, when looking at Zambia (which incidentally may achieve this MDG!), a lot of emphasis is put on enrolment, at the detriment of the *quality* of the education provided. I have been told that pupils at completion often still don't read nor speak English. Third, the attention for primary education went at the cost of secondary school, let alone higher education. Both are in a sorry state. As Clemens says, low levels of education beget low levels of development. The question arises: is the country preparing the young generation to take charge of Zambia's future development; would they be technically and intellectually equipped to take charge? I'm afraid not!

Regarding MDG 3: gender equality, this is measured by ratios of girls to boys in primary and secondary education. Now, if MDG 2 would be achieved, i.e. 100 % enrolment, then MDG 3 for primary school level would be redundant, since all boys *and* girls would be enrolled! Worldwide empirical evidence shows that girls are disproportionally affected, particularly in Sub-Saharan Africa. Yet, the actual female to male primary enrolment shows that Africa is doing better in terms of percentage changes than other regions. In other words, Africa is catching up to other developing countries in gender equality, but this is not measured by MDG 3.

What about MDG 4: reducing child mortality by two-thirds? This MDG is measured in percentage terms. Child mortality has been falling everywhere, including in Africa. Africa has shown a steady decline in child mortality from 260 in 1960 to 140 in 2005. Zambia's 2007 Demographic Health Survey confirmed this downward trend. This trend could have been even better, if Zambia would have done away with its perverse salary system, which induces staff to attend seminars, because of the sitting allowances involved, rather than attend to their core tasks.

Why then would Africa not meet MDG 4? Because the higher the initial mortality, the lower the subsequent percentage reduction in mortality. So, Africa is again short changed. The same applies to MDG 5 which measures the decrease of maternal mortality by two thirds. MDG 6 is concerned with halting and reversing the AIDS, TB and malaria epidemics. Again, the level of maternal mortality and the levels of AIDS, TB and malaria prevalence were higher in Africa than elsewhere; hence Africa's successes would be underplayed in the measurement of both MDG`s. What about MDG 7, the reduction of the number of people without clean water by half? This goal is negatively formulated: people *without access*; while the data collected measure the people *with access* to water. Would this MDG have been formulated in positive terms, it would show that Africa is catching up.

Because of the way the MDGs are measured, Africa fails to achieve them. This is doing injustice to what Africa achieved over the past decades. It may frustrate private foreign investments as the negative MDG outcomes would reinforce the stereotype that Africa always fails. The same might apply to aid. The opponents will say that aid doesn't help and thus should be slashed, which would be exactly the opposite of what the MDG'S intended to do for Africa!

(2009)

Moeletsi Mbeki's Sobering Views on Africa

During my student days there was a vibrant international debate about poverty and development. It was often ideologically inspired and a lot of contributors to that debate came from the 'South'. One of the first was Raul Prebisch who proposed import substitution, which was practiced a lot in South America and in some African countries at the time. Then, there was Frantz Fanon who wrote *The Wretched of the Earth*, a must-read book. Samir Amin wrote a book which we also had to read: *Imperialism and the Underdevelopment of Africa*. All this happened in the 1970's. After that there was silence from the 'South'. The development debate became monopolised by authors from the North and those from developing countries who had settled in Europe or America.

And now there is suddenly Dambisa Moyo whose *Dead Aid* became a best seller. Just recently another African, Moeletsi Mbeki (yes, Thabo's brother), wrote a polemic book entitled *Architects of Poverty*. Its subtitle is: *Why African Capitalism Needs Changing*.

His theme is that while Asia's internal conflicts after independence were resolved around 1965 (with the exception of Indochina) and the countries of East, South East and South Asia started on the second challenge: developing and diversifying their economies, Africa has still not resolved its conflicts. Mbeki points to Sudan, the tensions between Ethiopia and Eritrea, Rwanda's genocide and Ivory Coast's conflict. On the economic front, with very few exceptions, Africa's political elites have driven their countries' economies backward. Unlike Moyo, who points her finger to the donors, Mbeki puts the main blame for Africa's backwardness on conflicts and -especially- Africa's political elites. However, he does blame 'the donors' for supporting dictators who hindered the emergence of an independent middle class which could provide the leadership to drive Africa's desperately needed industrial and agricultural revolution.

The story of Africa today is the resurgence of the scramble for natural resources, this time by both West and East. Africa needs new rulers, says Mbeki, that is the people themselves who understand that the path to a

14

prosperous future lies in hard work, creativity, knowledge and equity.

Understandably, Mbeki illustrates his theme by referring a lot to South Africa's history, in particular the postapartheid era. Mbeki's analysis is sobering. For example he notes: 'The black upper middle class dominates the country's political life today but plays next to no role in the ownership and control of the productive economy of South Africa; its key role is overseeing the redistribution of wealth towards consumption. It manages (or should that be: mismanages?) a few state-owned enterprises inherited from the National Party era'. Mbeki explains the large (and growing) unemployment figure as a result of the negative effects of globalisation. South Africa now imports cheaper products than the local economy can produce. The manufacturing sector is thus getting smaller. Mbeki concludes that the gradual destruction of the manufacturing sector is at the root of growing impoverishment of South Africans. South Africa is sitting on a time bomb, as the country is creating a large and growing urban underclass, while the ruling elite is complacent and is not investing in adequate education, innovation and improvement of the country's productivity.

Zimbabwe's disgraceful decline is also mercilessly exposed by Mbeki. Apart from the human suffering and political brutalities, Zimbabwe's economy which was one of Africa's best, with a high degree of industrialization, is now only half the size it had in 2000. Life expectancy is the lowest in the entire world. Mbeki has little hope that Zimbabwe's present coalition government will bring improvements.

Looking back at Europe's and Asia's development, their internal conflicts have been sifted out, nation-states were moulded, and all the attention could be devoted to economic development. True, Mbeki's description of Asia's political and economic development is not correct (think of Afghanistan, Iraq, Kashmir, East Timor, Sri Lanka, Tibet, etc). But he is right in stating that a lot of Asian countries have *taken off*, which did not happen in the vast majority of African countries.

Now, why is that? Because, Mbeki says they consist of fossilised pre-industrial and pre-agrarian revolution social formations. The absence of an industrial revolution in Sub-Saharan Africa has left it with socio-economic structures that obstruct rather than promote growth and development. In fact, Sub-Saharan Africa, with a few exceptions, has *deindustrialized* since 1970. The author refers, amongst others, to Kafue in Zambia; once a hive of industrial activity. It had textile, fertilizer and chemical plants and a railway line that serviced them. There isn't much left of it.

Mbeki says that in order to develop you need institutions which provide the *incentives* to grow and leaders who ensure that these institutions function and deliver on expectations. Post colonial Africa has both failed to develop these institutions and to produce the leaders required to take society forward in the rapidly changing global environment.

The institutions that were left standing and prospered during the era of dictatorship and one-party rule were created by colonialism, i.e. the state, the military and police and the foreign controlled private sector.

The chapter on regional integration is called: *The failure of regional integration*. The question is: why should Sub-Saharan Africa integrate and why is it not working? Economic integration is supposed to benefit national economies; after all, broadening one's market provides more economic opportunities for export; moreover, imports from partner countries will be cheaper. Quite a few Sub-Saharan economies are simply too small to be economically viable on their own. Therefore, regional integration makes sense. There are many such regional integration bodies in Sub-Saharan Africa, with very little success so far because Africa does not have the material and political conditions for integration to work. For example, intra-SADC exports and imports dropped during the period 1992 - 2002.

It is the quality of domestic policies that will drive Africa's development, and *not* the way neighbour countries cooperate, says Mbeki. What will drive African economic development is the quality of relations between individual African countries and the world market. Mauritius is a good illustration of a small country that has followed the correct development model, exploiting world markets to develop its own industry.

In his concluding chapter Mbeki underlines that he only dealt with one factor that explains why Africa is not developing, that is the role played by

Africa's rulers. They have no sense of ownership of their country and are not interested in their development; on the contrary, it is in their interest to maintain the *status-quo*. More and more the spotlight is on them. Recent studies emphasize the frustrating role played by them, and just recently the Vatican condemned their poor performance.

If Africa is to develop it needs a new type of democracy and rulers; a democracy that will empower the private sector producers. In Africa most of them are peasants and they should be given land ownership which would encourage them to invest in land improvement. This new democracy should be able to restore the growth of an independent and productive middle class as well as facilitate the development of autonomous civil society institutions.

Mbeki mentions as signs of emerging new democracies the establishment of the MMD in Zambia and Zimbabwe's MDC. Although it is too early to pass a verdict, I don't see much change for the better happening in both countries. That brings me to my main criticism on Mbeki's otherwise thought provoking book. He concentrates his attention on the political elites who serve their own interests. Proper leadership is very important for a country to develop, but much more is required: high quality education, the rule of law, proper infrastructure, and a culture of entrepreneurship - just to mention a few other required factors- which leadership alone can't provide.

(2009)

Botswana, Africa's star grower

Botswana is one of 13 fast growing developing countries included in the World Bank's recent Growth Report. In fact Botswana is the only African country meeting the Report's criteria for inclusion in the top league of fast growers. These criteria are: economic growth at an average of 7 % a year for more than 25 years since 1950. Botswana indeed qualified convincingly.

Let us take a look at Botswana's growth record first before looking a bit deeper into the country's performance. Botswana experienced a staggering annual growth per capita of 13 % in the 1980's, starting from the same income level as Zambia at independence. Its long term growth, spanning the past four decades, was phenomenal, even surpassing that of the four Asian Tiger countries! Botswana's income per capita was 20 times higher in 2005 compared to its per capita income in 1960, while the Tigers' per capita income grew approximately 10 times during the same period. Botswana's income per capita is now seven times higher than Zambia's.

Well, the critical reader will observe, it is not so difficult to grow so fast if your country is the second largest diamond producer in the world and your population is small (1.9 million). The explanation for Botswana's success is that it established and managed to maintain a stable multi-party democracy since independence. Furthermore, Botswana was so fortunate to be governed by wise political leaders and -not least important- prudent economic policies.

Development economists think in models; they can be of the big push, the centre-periphery or the evolutionary variety, for example. Botswana's growth is food for thought for evolutionists. Now, what do they propose? They say that economic development is a process of successive upgrading, in which a nation's business environment evolves to support increasingly sophisticated and productive ways of competing.

As regards the process of growth, and more precisely for a country to move out of poverty, it must upgrade its inputs, institutions, and skills to allow more sophisticated forms of competition, resulting in increased

18

productivity. This, in turn, requires upgrading its human capital, improving infrastructure, promoting trade and foreign investment, protecting intellectual property, improving product quality and expanding regional integration. This sounds familiar, as it pretty much reflects the growth path taken by rich countries. This modernisation process was already captured in a simple model by the father of development economics, Arthur Lewis, way back in the early 1950s.

Lewis took as a starting point a pre-modern economy, where population is large relative to capital and natural resources and, consequently, there is a sheer unlimited supply of labour. As labour leaves the subsistence sector where marginal productivity is negligible, and moves into the capitalist sector with significantly higher productivity, structural change and economic modernisation will take place.

Is this process going on in Botswana? The answer is: not exactly. Despite its long period of growth Botswana is still mainly a primary product exporter. This does not mean that the verdict on Botswana should be altogether negative. Botswana is in many ways an exemplary state, whose political stability and management of its diamond wealth deserves admiration. Yet, the diversification of the economy has not taken place, and Botswana's wealth has not reached its poor population. Moreover, Botswana has one of the highest HIV/AIDS prevalence rates in the world. Let us take a closer look at these positive and less positive aspects.

Botswana is one of the most politically stable countries in Africa. After the retirement of President Masire in 1998, his successor, Festus Mogae, won a landslide victory both in 1999 and 2004. His successor, Ian Khama continued Botswana Democratic Party's uninterrupted and balanced rule ever since independence in 1966.

Botswana did not fall prey to the natural resource *trap*. The government nationalized all sub-soil mineral resources (read: diamonds) in 1967, the proceeds of which were well managed. A lot of natural resource abundant African countries did not manage their resources well. Instead of providing a source of investment capital, the profits were often pocketed by corrupt individuals or international companies, resulting in a negative correlation between natural resource endowments and economic growth.

Another danger posed by natural resources income is the so-called Dutch disease, which means that the currency of the country becomes over priced, triggering lower exports and inflation. What did Botswana do to prevent the curse and the Dutch disease? The government negotiated a 50-50 % deal with the De Beers mining company, ensuring significant resources revenues for the country. Diamonds now account for 42 % of the national income, 70 % of Botswana's exports and 50 % of government's income. The government has shown great care in the management of the diamond income, keeping expenses consistent in boom years and building up foreign exchange reserves to compensate for lean years. This strategy, combined with proper management of the exchange rate, has also meant that the value of the Pula (Botswana's currency) remained under control, which has been favourable for Botswana's exports. The income from diamond exports was invested in infrastructure, health and education as well as in international reserves ($10 billion).

Despite the prudent management of the diamond income, Botswana's mining sector presents a large disincentive for investments in other sectors: why invest in other sectors as long as he diamonds generate so much income? Moreover, investing in other sectors is hampered by skills shortages, weak administrative capacity, limited capacity of the construction sector, electricity shortages, high labour and transportation costs.

Botswana's agricultural sector is traditionally dominated by cattle rearing. Large herds are in the hands of few rich ranchers; small subsistence farmers don't have proper access to credit thereby perpetuating their poverty and low productivity. The traditionally strong connection between large cattle holders and government may well explain the reluctance to pass legislation favouring small holder farmers. As a result, quite a few poor farmers moved out of the sector into cities and towns, but this did not translate into a boost in productive activities.

Unemployment is high (18 %) and as long as the industrial and the service sectors are not expanding, unemployment will remain a major problem. All this has resulted in Botswana having one of the highest income inequalities in the world and 47 % of the population live below the poverty line. There are reports of ever increasing rural poverty.

The overlap between the wealthy, the political leaders and the bureaucracy explains the lack of interest in structurally addressing poverty. If this stalemate is not countered by new economic power holders, Botswana may not be able to transform itself from a growth power house and a primary product exporter into a state whose citizens benefit as evenly as possible from its wealth which can be sustained by a productive diversified economy. Hence, old economic elites have to be transformed or replaced, and the factors that hinder diversification have to be taken away, so that structural change and modernisation can take place.

(2008)

Why the Asian Tigers Grew so Fast

Many things from the past seemed so much simpler than today's. Take the old division between three 'worlds': the First World (roughly the rich countries), the Second World (The Soviet Union and other one-party, centrally planned countries), and the Third World, which emerged after former colonies gained independence. Now, the situation is a bit more complicated. Since the fall of the Berlin Wall the Second World has shrunk to a few *die hard* states, such as North Korea (where people die of hunger) and Cuba (from where 1 million Cubans fled). Also, the Third World has shrunk.

Many former third world countries have disintegrated into failing or failed states (quite a few in Africa), while others, especially in Asia, really took off in economic terms.

Understanding how these Asian countries grow so fast may be of help to Africa, to prevent it from 'missing the boat'.

In the 1950`s many South and East Asian countries had similar levels of income per capita as Africa's. The comparison between Zambia and South Korea comes to mind: both had the same income per head of $500 in 1960. Nowadays, Zambia is not much better off, while South Korea's income per capita is $20,400. And South Korea is not an exception: Singapore, Hong Kong, and Taiwan (together the Asian Tigers) achieved similar results over the past 4 decades. By the way, Japan preceded them, and Japan still is the second largest economy in the world after the United States. Runners-up are China and India, both huge economies and growing at break-neck speed.

Let us concentrate on the factors that explain the Asian Tigers´ growth. Interesting questions pose themselves, such as do their respective growth show a common pattern and what has government and the market's influence been? Lastly, did the attention for social welfare have the same priority?

As for growth, there is no such thing as one Asian growth strategy; each country had its distinct circumstances which triggered growth. Yet, there are some common aspects in the strategies applied, and all resulted in a tremendous improvement in living standards, in health care, in the quality of education and -last but not least- in overcoming poverty.

It was governments that took the lead in taking away the obstacles to the efficient operation of markets. The central question government policy makers asked themselves was how they could shape market forces so that they would promote industrial development.

Between the Asian Tigers, a distinction must be made between Hong Kong on the one hand and Singapore, South Korea and Taiwan on the other. Hong Kong was already a market economy as it traditionally left very much to the functioning of the market, with the exception of land (being government's main source of income) and housing. Hong Kong grew spectacularly: 6.2 % per annum over the past forty years. Its income per capita is now USD 26,000!

Singapore, like Hong Kong, started off as a free port city-state, but after it broke away from Malaysia, it soon became very much a state-run economy, in that it established its own companies such as the very successful Singapore Airlines. The government also promoted education policies to produce highly educated graduates to serve the demands of ever more sophisticated industries. This is probably the most important policy any government can apply: to provide the best possible education to prepare the country's *best and brightest* to take charge of its future development. What Singapore also did (and Hong Kong didn't at first), was to provide its population with housing at subsidised rates and to introduce a Central Pension Fund. Health care was also promoted by government. All these social welfare aspects demonstrate that Singapore successfully combined economic *and* social development; probably also explaining Singapore's political stability. Singapore registered an average growth rate of 7.7 % during the past 45 years, resulting in an income of U$ 27,000 per capita at present.

South Korea and Taiwan's growth stories are a bit different. Both applied an interventionist industrial policy, copied from their forerunner Japan. However, each country applied its own variety. Yet, both governments strongly promoted new industries, but not to control existing ones. The task of government planners was to identify which industries were most suited to the next stage of the country's development. In South Korea these decisions were made by a small group of technocrats located in the President's Office. After having identified the appropriate candidates for industrial development, the challenge then was to create the incentives for one of the large conglomerates *(chaebols)* to step in. These incentives consisted of offering infrastructure, subsidised loans from government banks, a monopoly over the domestic market and export subsidies. The government also invested heavily in the required education to supply these skills. In short, South Korea applied an infant industry strategy.

As for education, to this very day the Asian Tiger countries belong to the top-six in mathematics and science performance of 15-year olds of the International Student Assessment of the Organisation for Economic Cooperation and Development!

Contrary to South Korea, Taiwan's industrial policies were designed by senior civil servants. Taiwan's economy was not dominated by large conglomerates, such as South Korea's, but consisted of large numbers of small enterprises. Government initially relied, however, on state enterprises to implement their plans.

The Tigers´ industrialisation policies changed over time, reflective of their internal growth, of the changes within their political systems, and -of course- responding to the challenges of globalisation. And all went pretty fast! It is interesting to note that in the early 1960´s both South Korea and Taiwan were short of foreign exchange, which made them heavily rely on foreign aid, mainly from the United States. Hence, here we have a clear example of aid helping poor countries to grow.

Not having natural resources, both South Korea and Taiwan initially decided to promote exports of labour intensive manufacturing such as shoes and textiles. In the 1970´s a more sophisticated phase of industrial development started through the promotion of the heavy and chemical industry. In the 1980s political opposition emerged through a rising middle class and an activist student body, forcing an end to authoritarian rule and the beginning of pluralistic politics. Information technology came up as a fresh challenge in the early 1990s. New industries were created and Taiwan, for example, revamped its tertiary education system so that it could produce the skills needed for the new technology. It created a science park to lure Taiwanese engineers and scientists back to the island!

Partly because of pressure from the United States to lower their import tariffs and partly because the lesser need for protecting their industries, the Tigers gradually opened up their economies to the outside world.

With the exception of Singapore, the other Tigers did not pay much attention to social welfare. They were catching up later. South Korea and Taiwan are now providing pensions plus publicly supported education and health care.

Looking back, the Tigers' policies were clearly promoting industrial development, following Japan's example. All were very successful. Their rapid economic growth produced a growing and highly educated middle class that not only provided a highly competent work force, but also got tired of authoritarian rule and demanded better social policies.

Zambia's economic prospects are good. Copper prices will continue to be high for the foreseeable future. Proceeds from agriculture and tourism contribute more and more to the urgently needed diversification of the economy, making it more robust and resilient against external shocks. But more is needed to ensure substantial and *sustained* economic growth to achieve its intended middle-income status by 2030. The Asian Tigers demonstrated that rapid and sustained economic growth can be done. How they did it serves as an inspiration for Zambia's policy makers.

(2008)

Latin America's Economic Stagnation

Debates about poverty and development nowadays focus on poor Africa and fast growing Asia. Latin America has disappeared from the scene. It is not poor enough to attract attention, nor does its low growth attract foreign investors. Latin America is the *Forgotten Continent* in the development debate.

After almost 200 years of independence, Latin America has not been able to achieve levels of economic development comparable to, for example, the fast growing Asian countries. How come? After all, they have had much more time to shed their colonial heritage, build up their own human capital and to achieve growth and prosperity. True, Argentina and Venezuela were amongst the richest countries on earth at the beginning and at the middle of the 20th century respectively! Yet, they slid back. What it takes to achieve high standards of living is a growth rate of at least 8 %, which is to be *sustained* over a long period of time. Chile is now the only Latino country which has the potential to sustain its growth and converge with the rich world.

This is how Latin America fared compared to others. In the early part of the 19th century, Latin America was considered the richest region of what is now called the developing world. Its average income was, however, half of that of the USA. After most Latin American countries gained independence in the 1820's, growth did not pick up, as a result of political turmoil and internal warfare.

During the first wave of globalisation (1870 - 1914) Latin America started to grow: on average 1.8 % per year, benefitting from high demand for its export products. But after the crash of Wall Street in 1929, Latin America started to look inward and its growth petered out. During the second wave of globalisation (1950 - 1973) growth picked up again, but it was four times smaller than, for example, Japan's. East Asia converged since that period with the rich world, but Latin America failed to do that.

There is no one overarching explanation for Latin America's stagnation. There are quite a few, ranging from its colonial heritage, dictatorships, high inequality, mistaken import substitution policy, low quality of education, and poor institutional development.

Latin America has the most unequal income distribution in the world. This has historic and ethnic origins. The Spanish and Portuguese colonisers established large agricultural plantations (*haciendas*) owned by them. The indigenous population was left with less fertile land, resulting in a highly uneven land distribution and ditto income distribution. Loads of slaves were imported from Africa to work on these plantations and in the silver mines. Slavery was only abolished in Brazil for example at the end of the 19th century. Moreover, the Indian indigenous population was discriminated against (it must be noted that the indigenous Indian population of North America was almost wiped out altogether). Even now these influences shine through the figures: the richest 10% of the population takes between 34 and 47 % of the income depending on the country, while the poorest 20 % get only 5%. Although most Latin American countries are officially classified as middle income, almost 40% of Latin Americans (or 205 million people) still live below the poverty line. Economists have found that inequality in income is a strong hindrance to growth and that is one explanation of Latin America's stagnation.

Another prominent explanation for Latin America's failure to converge is the ill-conceived *import substitution* policy, promoted by CEPAL, the UN Economic Commission for Latin America, in the early 1950s. It was its first Secretary-General, Raul Prebisch, who fathered this policy, inspired by a Marxist explanation of why some countries were rich and Latin America remained poor. It went as follows: Latin America suffered from a structural decline in its terms of trade; its exports of primary products got even cheaper because a surplus of labour held down wages, whilst its imports of manufactures from rich countries became more expensive because productivity gains were pocketed by increasingly monopolistic industrial firms rather than passed on as lower prices. Hence, free trade would not bring Latin America the surplus capital required to industrialise. Instead, governments should intervene to promote internal industrialisation through protective tariffs, subsidised credit and with the state itself setting up basic industries where private initiative could not or would not.

This widely applied policy has had disastrous effects, not only because it failed, but it also has led to uncompetitive firms, low productivity, high inflation, and indebtedness. Neither did it trigger a higher quality of education, which to this day is still inadequate to help Latin America's industries to become more competitive. By the way, better education will definitely also help diminish the gap between the rich and poor.

The Asians applied a much more effective industrialisation policy. True, they initially also protected their nascent industries behind tariff walls, but their policies were not inward looking to substitute imports as Latin America's; no, they were export-led, with smashing success!

What governments in many Latin American countries also failed to do was to reform the role of the state and their public institutions. The state is still supposed to perform many tasks, its regulations are cumbersome. For example, it takes ten months to register a small tailoring shop in Peru. Latin America's civil services are typically bloated and littered with incompetent people. Public institutions which ought to be independent or autonomous, such as the Judiciary and the Auditor-General, are not always; appointments of judges and the Auditor-General are often politically inspired; merit considerations play second fiddle.

In many ways, Latin America is no longer the most advanced region of the developing world, as it was in the 1960s. It has obviously lost out to the fast growing Asian countries demonstrating much higher levels of productivity than Latin America can boast of. Its wage levels are much higher than those of China for example in basic manufacturing. Moreover, and worrying at that, Latin America's educational levels are no better than those of China; they are worse than South Korea's , and the region lacks India's large numbers of English-speaking graduates (think of all the call centres there of American and European credit card companies, airlines, hotels and travel agencies). Latin America's main advantage in low value added manufacturing is its proximity to the United States´ market.

Given its history, will Latin America ever change for the better? There are signs that it may. It has shed dictatorships, democratically elected governments are the norm (Cuba is the only exception), be it that some presidents apply populist policies, such as Hugo Chavez in Venezuela and Evo Morales in Bolivia. Yet, most are moderate: neither purely capitalist nor socialist. The past few years, inflation has been conquered and economic growth has picked up again, and quite a few Latin American companies have entered the list of the Boston Consulting Group's 100 largest multinationals from emerging economies. 13 Brazilian companies appear on that list and from Mexico there are seven. The most prominent amongst them are the cement producer Cemex from Mexico, and CVRD (mining) and Embraer (midsize passenger jets) from Brazil.

Many governments are addressing the problem of poverty through social protection schemes. Successes have been achieved in Brazil, Chile, Argentina and Mexico. This is not to say that poverty has been eradicated, yet if the economic growth can be sustained and more jobs and better education can be provided, Latin America may shed its turbulent history of coups, warfare, erratic economic performance, and join those developing countries that are catching up with the rich countries. Time will tell whether Latin America will be able to sustain its upward development or that it will revert to stagnation as so often in its past.

(2008)

DEVELOPMENT

To What Society Does one Belong?

The other day I met a lady who has lived in Zambia for more than 40 years. We were talking about Zambia's development; my favourite subject by the way. It used to be hers, as she said: 'Zambians are sitting on a pot of gold, so to speak, but they don't seem to recognise it. Why is it that their potential wealth hasn't been tapped? I don't know. I have given up finding an explanation'. The income of the average Zambian hasn't improved much since independence. True, there are now many more Zambians (approx. 12 million) compared to 1964 when there were only 2.8 million but other poor countries' populations have also grown and still were able to boost their growth. The question is thus: what makes an economy tick, and -not least important- what factors *block* growth?

I came across the interesting World Bank study *Limited Access Orders in the Developing World* which analyses stagnation and growth, lead-authored by Douglass North, economic historian and winner of the Nobel Prize for Economics in 1993. North and his co-authors identify three types of societies. The simplest type is the primitive order society (the hunter-gatherer one), followed by the limited access order society and the open access order society. Since mankind has left the primitive order society largely behind it, the study focuses on the limited access order society and the open access variety.

I should mention that North's study was inspired by the realization that most development policy today is based on models of the developed world and donors' attempts to make developing countries look like the developed ones. And that doesn't work, at least not in the majority of poor African countries. Why is it that so few development approaches were successful?

There is apparently a serious mismatch between theory and practice. North responds by stating that the social and above all- the political dynamics of developed countries are fundamentally different from those of developing countries. Development policies often fail because they try to transplant elements of the open access order such as competition, markets and democracy, directly into the limited access orders (LAOs). These policies threaten the privileged position of the elites in control and challenge the very logic on which the limited access order society is organized.

Attempts to remove corruption, create the rule of law, and institute democracy with competitive parties can destabilize an LAO and generate resistance from those in control. Paradoxically, many who are exploited by these policies will hesitate to push for reform because they see disorder and violence as worse than being exploited economically.

Thus, the first step to more effective development policies is to better understand how societies actually behave and how developing societies are different from developed ones. In doing so, North and his co-authors developed the three types of societies I just mentioned.

The *limited access order society* bars access to valuable political and economic functions to generate income for the elites in control. The status-quo is maintained by this privileged group through controlling violence (which otherwise undermines their power) and by maintaining stability. But there is more: LAOs also frustrate the creation of organizations of potentially competing groups in society. In other words, we are talking about a society which deliberately closes off political and economic possibilities for others than the happy few. Relations between those in power and all others are personalized, says North, such that the delivery of government services depends on whom the recipient is connected to. North concludes that the administration of welfare programs, business licenses, etc, all require personal exchange and often bribes. To sum up: LAOs typically have state-controlled industries, problematic business licensing regimes, and corrupt patron-client networks. They are not necessarily stable societies; the composition of the coalition in power may change, but they remain LAOs.

In contrast, the *open society order* allows *all* citizens access to economic, political, and social organisations; so, all can participate in a society's economic, social and political domain. The open access society relies on competition, the free creation of organisations representing the interests of particular groups to hold the society together. North notes that in the open access order society economic dynamism is created precisely because undertaking economic activities is open to all entrepreneurs.

Tackling the problem of development within LAOs is unlikely to succeed simply by transplanting open access institutional forms and mechanisms. But then the question is: what instead? Can an LAO *leap frog* into an open access order (OAO) society? After all, many elites in LAOs have been educated in Europe and North America, and many bring back ideas of institutional models from where they have studied. Modern technology is available to hem as well; just think of the tremendous possibilities provided by the Internet and mobile phones. Yet corporations, parliaments, the judiciary, etc. which have been established in many developing countries do operate differently when surrounding economic and cultural situations are different. And growth due to technological change does not necessarily produce open access order societies. For example, once the internet becomes a threat, such as the recent *Google case* in China, the LAO state blocks it.

Many LAO's have dualistic economies with a domestic economy governed by domestic rules and institutions on the one hand, and international enclaves run by OAO rules and institutions on the other. LAO elites gain from this duality as it gives them the opportunity to prosper without having to bother about the development of their domestic economy. African authors, such as Moeletsi Mbeki, come to the same observation in his *Architects of Poverty*.

Now where does Zambia fit? North is not very flattering about Zambia and comparable states. He wrote: 'Elites in failed or miserably performing states today can stay in power with financing from various combinations of foreign military and economic assistance and sales of natural resources such as those of Bolivia, Surinam, Guyana, Nigeria, Zambia , Pakistan, etc. '

All his doesn't imply that LAO's would all be stagnant poor economies. No, says North, the great civilizations of the past were all successful limited access orders. LAOs include a wide variety of societies: The Roman Republic and Empire, Britain under the Tudors, and all low and middle-income countries are LAOs. But one thing they have in common is that all of them manipulate the economy to produce income and wealth for the elite. History has also demonstrated that the path from an LAO to an OAO society is not a one-way street; there are examples of OAO's sliding back to an LAO status.

Tipping points

What I find most interesting is that in comparing limited access order societies to the open access one we can better understand what makes the limited access order graduate into an open society order. After all, that is what development -and aid in particular- is all about. The *'tipping point'* comes when open access in the economic or political domain results in sufficient power of the new entrants to press the elites, who are in control, to accept them. These elites give in when they conclude that their interests are better served by allowing the new entrants in and by supporting intra-elite competition. Once this stage is reached, history demonstrates that rapid and fundamental changes occur extending to ever larger segments of society.

In mature LAOs, North explains, sophisticated private organisations begin to emerge and their independence from the state becomes more clearly defined. And mature LAO states must create new institutions that provide services (such as sophisticated skills training) for these new organisations, including the protection of their property rights. Once erstwhile elite rights are defined impersonally, it may be possible to extend those rights to a wider circle of society. History tells us that once this happened, new incentives to tap the wealth of non-elites arose. North's access model indicates that the tipping point comes when open access in one dimension (economic or political) commands sufficient power to press successfully for open access to the other dimension.

This sounds fine from a theoretical perspective, but how did the tipping points emerge in real development trajectories? Let's take South Korea's example. This country had more or less the same income per capita in the 1950s as Zambia's. Now, what did South Korea do since? It applied a rigorous interventionist industrialisation policy, copied from its forerunner Japan, promoted by its political leaders and managed by a small group of very capable technocrats located in the President's office. Large industrial conglomerates were formed *(chaebols)* and incentives were provided to them by way of free infrastructure, tax breaks, subsidized loans from government banks, a monopoly over the domestic market and export subsidies. The government also invested heavily in education to supply the required skills. In short, South Korea applied a very successful infant industry policy. Needless to say that these infants eventually became mature, sophisticated industrial giants, such as Samsung and Hyundai. And South Korea evolved from a dictatorship into a democracy.

The beauty of North's distinction in access order societies is that it helps to better understand why societies function as they do; what factors block development and what other factors broaden the economic and political playing field. North -as so many other development thinkers- does not give practical suggestions what should be done in real life terms to have an LAO ' tip' into an open access order society. That is to be sorted out in each particular society I guess, dictated by its specific political, economic and cultural features. However, without a sustained developmental vision for the medium to long term by a country's leadership, combined with a rigorous implementation, many African LAOs will not mature.

(2010)

Is Understanding Development Difficult?

Economists are struggling with this question. I don't know why, because when one looks at the economic development of successful countries it is fairly easy to detect what the factors have been which made them grow. The trouble which economists face is that they try to put all these factors in one universal growth model. And that has -so far- proven to be beyond their reach, as economics alone cannot capture the variety of factors at play: political, social, historical, cultural, geographic, you name it. So, the challenge -as I see it- is to put all of them in one dynamic growth model, and *presto!* the universal growth model emerges!

Let me share with you what factors explain the development of high income countries. Around 1500 AD North Western European countries started to increase their agricultural productivity. Moreover, European discoverers ranging from Vasco da Gama, Magelhanes, Abel Tasman, and most famous of the lot: Columbus, opened up the rest of the world for Europe's economic and political gains. The resulting introduction of precious metals (gold and silver from Latin America) and precious consumer goods such as tea, sugar, spices, and tobacco promoted international trade, boosted consumption and urbanization.

I must add that the Chinese undertook discovery voyages a century *earlier* than the Europeans to explore the waters of Indonesia and the Indian Ocean. China was far more advanced in technological terms at that time. But in 1477 China turned away from the sea and started to look inward, for a very long time by the way.

One development led to another. The increase in commerce and trade triggered the growth of urban commercial centres in the 17th century (such as Amsterdam and London) and the increase in literacy and numeracy. Science started to flourish and technological inventions promoted industrial productivity, starting in Britain in the early 19th century, but soon followed by the European continent. This economic dynamism blew over across the Atlantic to North America and later to Australia and New Zealand.

At the beginning of the 20th century Japan started to modernise. Its example was followed by by the Four Asian Tigers (South Korea, Taiwan, Singapore and Hong Kong), and in their slip stream by China and India. Other Asian countries such as Malaysia, Indonesia, Thailand, and Vietnam are runners up.

The question is: what about the rest of the world? Where do most of Latin America, the Arab world and Sub-Saharan Africa appear in the league of successful countries? That is a good question, showing the other side of the growth coin: persistent stagnation. Many explanations have been proffered, such as geographical location; after all most of the rich countries are to be found in the temperate zones. Max Weber explained growth by pointing at cultural factors: the protestant ethic would have it that people work hard, be curious, study, save and invest, aiming to improve their life. Other scholars point at the role of institutions; they provide the *incentives* for growth, or the disincentives for it. Then, there are those who emphasize the political realties in societies. They distinguish two types of societies: the *open access order* society, in which the political and economic dynamics reinforce each other. And there is the *limited access order* society in which the elites reap most benefits, not allowing other sections of society to share; a sure recipe for poverty and stagnation. Yet others, when looking at countries endowed with a rich reservoir of natural resources, explain stagnation as a result of the *natural resource curse*. This means that the proceeds from oil, diamond or copper aren't reinvested in the country to, for example, diversify the economy, but are channeled into Swiss bank accounts and into the coffers of multinationals.

The trouble with all these theories is that none of them is universally applicable; there are always exceptions. Take Botswana, it is well endowed with diamond deposits. But no natural resource curse. Botswana was the fastest growing country in the world during the past four decades. And many successful South East Asian countries are located in the tropics and not in the temperate zones.

What made them grow so spectacularly, while many of them were poorer than Zambia in the 1960s? South East Asia registered almost continuous economic growth over the past 45 years. In Africa per capita income stagnated in the 1970s, declined a decade later, grew weakly in the 1990s, and in 2005 it was still lower than it had been in 1975. Sub-Saharan Africa remained dependent on exporting raw materials which are sensitive to the volatility of the world market. Subsistence farming remains a key source of livelihood in most countries, and whatever there was of manufacturing, that virtually collapsed since the 1980s.

True, Sub-Saharan Africa's economies are growing, but the growth is mainly based on international demand for its commodities, such as copper and oil. A very narrow base, I'd say, and combined with the low productivity of agriculture and other employment-generating sectors (e.g. tourism), this leaves few possibilities to respond to adverse trade shocks. A recent World Bank study concluded that, given the deterioration of public institutions and social service delivery over the past two decades, more than half of Sub-Saharan Africa's countries risk a substantial increase in poverty.

In the 1960's this was predicted about Asia's fate, and we know that these predictions were wrong. So what did many Asian countries do? By and large, the successful growers applied a consistent policy with the sole aim to leave poverty behind by boosting economic growth. The main ingredients were state-led agricultural development and industrialisation.

The policies concerned translated into raised rural incomes, which -in turn-reduced mass poverty. Subsequently, a sound environment for industrial development was created. By the way, investing in rural areas where the mass of the poor at the time lived was also done to stem the 'voice' of political opposition (as we have recently seen cropping up in Thailand). All this went hand in hand with sound macroeconomic policies.

In contrast, investments in Sub-Saharan Africa are mainly in mining and other extractive industries, which are typically capital intensive and require little labour. These investments have few linkages with the domestic economy, so that the multiplier effect is limited.

Asia's investment in rural/agricultural development typically implemented by highly competent technocrats, combined growth with poverty reduction, whilst Africa invested in mining which did little to bring

39

poverty down. Take Malaysia: when it was already becoming an industrial power, the government was still spending 25 % of its development budget on agriculture!

Would this be the way forward for Zambia? There is a lot going for it, I'd say. After all, Zambia avails of a huge reservoir of agricultural potential. Its soil is rich, water for irrigation abounds, agro-processing can be developed. Jobs will be created, farmers incomes will increase, poverty which is most persistent in rural areas, will be reduced. On top of this, a thriving agricultural sector would make Zambia less dependent on copper and ensure food security.

This suggestion isn't new. Economic advisers have suggested this for ages. Hopefully, the Sixth National Development Plan (2011-2015) will map out a policy to diversify the economy, starting with the agricultural sector and, which is another big challenge, effectively implement that policy.

Whatever the case may be the recipe for growth is simple: hard work, exploiting the country's resources, entrepreneurship, a lean and mean government capable of implementing a clear development policy sustained over a long time, a well trained workforce, a strong voice of the population, and an adequate physical and telecommunications infrastructure - in short, a collective wish and attitude to exploit Zambia's tremendous economic possibilities, which will help achieving its goal of becoming a middle-income country by 2030.

(2010)

Recipes for disaster or growth?

The other day I was invited to a party whose guests I didn't know. Needless to say that, neither did they know me. When chatting a bit, I was asked what I had studied. Development economics, I said, which triggered the reaction: Oh, but then you must know how development and growth comes about! I thought: 'Oops; that is a tough one', because development economics does not really explain what factors explain economic growth. Lots of theories have seen the light, but none has proven to be universally applicable, so far.

The beginning of development economics coincided with the large wave of many developing countries gaining independence after the Second World War. Before that, there was colonial economics and -of course- conventional economics which also dealt with growth models. Development economics, however, became a special field, focusing on the question how poor developing countries could eradicate poverty and have their economics converge with those of rich countries.

After the end of the Second World War there was a sense of optimism in the Western world. The Marshall Plan successfully helped Europe back on its feet in five years. It was thought that reconstruction and development could be done rather quickly! Inspired by that spirit Walt Rostow presented his famous five stages of economic growth. His theory ran as follows: developing countries are in short supply of capital to finance investments which in turn promote development. These countries initially also lack the knowledge and talents to make these investments productive. Hence, they should be helped with capital and technical assistance to economically *take off*, after which they would gradually evolve into Rostow's final stage of self-sustained growth.

Unfortunately, it did not work out like that for many poor countries, as we know by now. But what was it that kept them poor? They were trapped in poverty and they were facing a financing gap, it was thought. Poor countries are poor and therefore cannot generate the capital to invest into productive activities, and that is why they remain poor. That sounds logical;

41

however, if this reasoning would be correct, there would not be rich countries. After all, the rich countries were all very poor before they started to grow. Furthermore, not all investments lead to growth. Take Zambia: if it had converted all the billions of aid dollars into productive investments, Zambia should now have a per capita income of USD 20,000 as William Easterly has calculated. As a matter of fact, Zambia's income per capita is lower than it was at independence in 1964; the poverty rate is high at 64 %. At independence the country's income level was 75 % above the African average income. Today, Zambia's per capita income is below that of the African average.

There are also theories which don't look at growth, but try to explain why poverty is perpetuated. The *Dependencia theory* was very popular in the 1960's and 1970's, especially in Latin America. It was based on Marxist principles. Its rationale runs as follows: poor countries suffer from a structural decline in their terms of trade. Its export of primary products get cheaper because a surplus of labour holds down wages, whilst its import of manufacturers from rich countries becomes more expensive because productivity gains are protected by increasingly monopolistic industrial firms, rather than passed on as lower prices. The dependencia theory was widely accepted by Latin American policy makers, who thought that import substitution was the appropriate antidote for dependence. It proved not to be, with disastrous effects for many Latin American economies.

In the early decades of development economics it was believed that the State should play a prominent role in the growth of a country as it was assumed that developing countries did not have a reliable market price system and that entrepreneurship was still limited. The state was seen as the principle agent of change. In many African countries this belief was put into practice, strongly promoted by the policies of aid giving countries. As it happened, state-led development did not promote growth; it resulted in sharp economic decline and impoverishment in Africa. I believe that the state-led development philosophy has been one of the biggest tragedies of young African nations, including Zambia.

After the first oil crisis in 1973, a sharp change in growth thinking occurred, as the growth models applied did not bring growth, nor did they create employment. The dramatic change concerned the re-appreciation of the functioning of the market, which in the past was greatly hindered by state intervention. It was high time, so it was thought, to *get the prices right*; a central theme of neo-classical economics. Zambia followed suit, after the near collapse of its economy, by opening up to privatisation and allowing market forces to play their part. That happened in the early 1990's, when unfortunately copper prices were very low, and the mines were sold off at very low prices.

But to get the prices and the policies right, it was also very necessary, economic analysts discovered, to get the institutions right. The institutional dimension was introduced in the 1980's by Nobel laureate Douglass North, who observed that in real life there are no perfectly functioning markets; a basic assumption of the neo-classicists. Their theory cannot, for example, explain the persistence of long periods of inefficient forms of exchange; of stagnation in other words. North introduced the relevance of institutions, which -together- form the incentive structure of societies. And it is incentives that explain to a large extent whether people and firms are willing to invest or not, and whether entrepreneurship is being promoted, But, as North himself confessed in 2001, we know a good deal of what makes for successful development (namely a favourable institutional framework), but we very little about how to get there.

Since then, more growth research has been done, and political science was brought in, adding the important interaction between economic and political institutions. The research results demonstrate, on the basis of the evolution of e.g. the Dutch and British economy and society, how economic institutions (which shape economic outcomes) are determined by political power, which in turn is determined by political institutions. I think that the study of the interplay between economic and political institutions is very helpful to better understand the long-term process of growth.

But in promoting Zambia's growth now, hands-on recipes are urgently needed. Harvard's Dani Rodrik provides them. He suggests to take away the binding constraints that inhibit economic growth. His reasoning is that in the past too little attention was paid to stimulating the dynamic forces that would unleash growth. Moreover, past growth experiences suggest that policymakers interested in igniting growth may be better served by targeting the most binding constraints of economic growth, rather than by investing scarce capacities in ambitious institutional reforms. And, as he rightly adds, different countries require different solutions to overcome their particular constraints. I like Rodrik's advice as it is focussing on the most essential factor to help overcome poverty: economic growth. Secondly, he rejects a 'one size fits all' approach to development, which has not worked.

Now, what would these binding constraints be in the case of Zambia, which possesses quite a lot of economic potential in mining, in farming and in tourism, to name a few? One doesn't have to study Zambia in depth to identify poor access to domestic and international markets as a formidable constraint. Uncompetitive production costs and low productivity are others. Poor infrastructure is also not helpful; we are all familiar with intermittent power cuts and the poor condition of roads. Technical and university education are not yet geared to the needs of industrial firms. One should also not overlook the ongoing appreciation of the kwacha which adversely affects Zambia's exports. If the Government were to successfully take away these constraints Zambia's economic future will look much brighter.

(2008)

The World Bank's Growth Report

Last year I read in *The Economist* that the World Bank had taken the initiative to request a distinguished group of scholars and development practitioners to answer the question what we know about economic growth. I found it a very good initiative, as even the most recent and sophisticated economic growth theories don't provide the universal answer to that question. The Bank appointed Nobel laureate Michael Spence to lead a Commission of 19 theoreticians and practitioners to look into the question. The Commission presented its report a few months ago and this article is about its contents.

The Commission selected 13 successful developing countries to analyse what factors would explain their growth. Each of them had registered growth at an average of 7 % a year for more than 25 years since 1950. That left out many poor countries which at times grew fast but could not maintain it, and fell back to economic stagnation. Sustained high growth is not easy; if it were, the list of successful developing countries would undoubtedly be longer.

The 13 lucky ones are: Botswana (the only qualifying African country), Brazil, China, Hong Kong, Indonesia, Japan, South Korea, Malaysia, Malta, Oman, Singapore, Taiwan, and Thailand. I wondered why Japan was included, as it was already well underway to become a developed country before 1950. But who am I to challenge the Commission's wisdom?

Each of these countries grew faster than any country before them. That was possible, notes the Report, because the world economy is now more open and integrated. This allows for fast-growing economies to import ideas, technologies, and knowhow from the rest of the world. Since learning something is easier than inventing it, fast learners can rapidly close the gap with the leading economies. Sustainable high growth is catch-up growth; and the global economy is the essential resource. This also applies to demand. The internal market of most developing countries is just too small to rely exclusively on domestic demand to sustain its growth. That is why most successful developing countries benefitted greatly from export-led growth.

The Report concluded that each of the 13 fast growing countries has its specific characteristics and historical experiences that explain their economic success. Nonetheless, they all share common characteristics: all of them form part of the global economy, maintain macro-economic stability, stimulate saving and investment, provide market-oriented incentives, and are reasonably well governed. Moreover, the governments of the 13 high growth countries were not free market purists. Their governments tried a variety of interventionist policies to help diversify their exports or sustain competitiveness. They included industrial policies to promote investments in new sectors, and managed exchange rates (such as China!). Most of them neglected protecting the environment in the early stages of their development.

The Report does not provide *the* answer to the growth question, as no generic formula exists. Based on the different growth paths taken by the 13 successful ones, the Report concluded that any growth policy choice to be made should be context and country specific! This is an important deviation from previous (Bank) thinking. In the past, universal policy advice was given. The paradigm of the past two decades was the Washington Consensus which included the liberalisation of trade, deregulation of prices, the privatisation of public enterprises, right-sizing the public sector, and restoration of monetary stability. It did not bring about the hoped for sustained growth, not even in countries which applied the prescribed policy rigorously, such as, for example, Bolivia. Yet, it must be admitted that the structural adjustment programs introduced in quite a few near bankrupt Sub-Saharan African and Latin American countries in the last decades of the past century, were not only very necessary but did also help restore macroeconomic and monetary stability in many.

The Report's subtitle is: *Strategies for Sustained Growth and Inclusive Development*. Hence, due attention is paid to the redistributive element of growth and -in particular- to the fight against poverty. What insights on fighting poverty does the Report give us? Relying on markets, the report notes, to allocate resources efficiently is necessary (as there is no effective substitute), but it is not the same thing as letting some combination of markets and a menu of reforms determine who will benefit from growth. After all, if large numbers of people don't feel any improvement in their income compared to others, there is clearly more work to be done to have the poor share a larger share of the pie. The Report says that what governments can do to protect people from poverty is to educate them and to teach them new skills when the evolving economy requires them. Another policy is a package of social protection, already widely applied in various Latin American countries, as governments realize that without it, popular support for their growth policies will erode.

When implementing policies, governments should rely on an effective public sector. That seems an *open door* remark. But the public sector of the typical poor country is overstaffed, underpaid, often prone to corruption, and not capable of retaining talented staff.

Government, however, is not the main driver of growth; that role belongs to the private sector, to investment and entrepreneurship responding to market forces. But an effective government is a must in underscoring sustained growth. The question is not about which actor is the most important to promote growth; or which one comes first: investing in better health and education or in business enterprises? They go hand in hand and, in the process, reinforce each other; investing in healthier and better educated people does not crowd out private investment, it crowds it in! A thriving private sector in turn triggers the supply of a broad range of skilled people, and provides the extra (tax) income for government to invest in better education, infrastructure, and health. These three public investments are basic for private sector development. And that is where most Sub-Saharan countries still fall short; roads, public buildings, power stations and the like are often in disrepair; education and health services are often of poor quality. There is a lot of mileage to be gained.

The Report is especially addressed to four types of countries that face particular challenges in achieving sustained high growth: African countries, small states, countries rich in natural resources, and middle-income countries. Hence, the Report applies on two counts for Zambia, being African and natural resource-rich. The way forward to achieve sustained growth is raising investments, diversifying the export base, whilst as rapidly as possible increasing employment opportunities, increasing the economy's (agricultural) productivity, establish regional economic cooperation, reducing the cost of doing business supported by public investment in infrastructure, better schooling and fostering a healthy population. As for Zambia's copper, the Report offers the following advice: Capture an appropriate share of the resource; save a reasonable amount overseas, and set clear, growth-oriented priorities so as to absorb the remainder at home. Zambia has rightly signed up to the Bank's recent Extractive Industries Transparency Initiative (its EITI ++ program) which assists countries to manage their resource wealth through (i) help in the design of auctions, (ii) monitor royalty collections, and (iii) provides guidelines about how much to spend and how much to save.

For those familiar with recent insights in development, the Report does not provide new vistas. It concentrates on the factors explaining growth and redistribution. The Report underscores that there are no universal approaches to growth; each country requires its specific policies. Inspired by China's successful step by step approach, the Report also advocates this: it is better to test a policy out first before applying it across the board. As I believe that the Report contains many recommendations which are relevant for Zambia's future development, the Report deserves the attention of policymakers, researchers, think tanks, media people and donor representatives.

(2008)

PUBLIC SECTOR REFORM

Government's Efforts to Perform Better

Now that Zambia's presidential elections are over, I thought it is interesting to write about civil service reform, which is not often hitting newspapers' headlines. This is understandable, but also strange. Understandable, because civil service reform is not very exciting; strange, because a well functioning civil service is absolutely vital for the development of any country, Zambia included. And that does not only apply to providing social services such as health, education and the building of roads; it also applies to regulating the markets; the failure to do so triggered the crisis of the international financial markets.

Let me start with the origin of civil service reform in Africa. When many Sub Saharan Africa countries were on the border of financial collapse in the 1980's, civil service reform was put at centre stage in negotiations between them and the IMF and World Bank, who both were called in to help. The Bank and the IMF prescribed Structural Adjustment Programs (SAPs), which were designed to restore macroeconomic order and to *downsize* the civil service in order to bring the wage bill under control, which was typically governments' single largest expenditure item.

These SAP's were not very popular, as they were perceived as cruel to Africa's poor. What SAP critics did not acknowledge was that many African (and Latin American, I should add) governments had been responsible for creating bloated, ineffective and -above all- unaffordable civil services. The *wage bill* of many governments at the time ate up often more than 90 % of government's budget. Hence, there were no funds to invest in roads, schools and hospitals, which were increasingly financed through foreign loans. Government debts grew so big that quite a lot of African countries could not repay them and became effectively bankrupt. Most of the countries who received help from the IMF and the Bank restored macroeconomic stability. Civil service reform, including Zambia's, was not successful.

This failure is now better understood, as drastically cutting the wage bill did not take into account the very limited job opportunities outside the public sector, the political culture to reward political parties' supporters with government jobs, the complex nature of civil service reform, limited implementing capacity and, last but not least, most African governments lacked the political commitment to implement civil service reform. Moreover, practice has shown that the so-called *big bang* approach (i.e. many civil servants sacked in one go) did not work.

Since the first generation of civil service reforms was introduced in the 1980s, a lot of thinking on the role of the state has happened. Firstly, the minimalist state philosophy (as advocated strongly by then USA President Ronald Reagan and UK's Prime Minister Margaret Thatcher), made way for a more balanced view of the role of the state: Governments are not only there to provide health, education, roads, etc., they should also correct market failures and create an environment to promote private sector development. Hence, a fresh philosophy on the role of the state emerged, being a complementary mix of state and market which would be best for the creation of sustained economic development. The thinking about civil service reform also evolved from the original downsizing to rightsizing. It was no longer felt that large numbers of civil servants should go. No, an appropriate number *and* quality of civil servants would be required for the state to play its part well. This would be best achieved when the civil service would become more efficient, effective, transparent and accountable. This, again, was easier said than done. Many African countries tried but most were not very successful.

Zambia embarked on a reform programme in 1993 which included rightsizing, pay reform and performance management. It was called the Public Sector Capacity Building Project; PSCAP in short. How did PSCAP fare? The number of Zambian civil servants fell from 180,000 in 1993 to 139,000 in 1997 and went further down to 104,000 in 2000. But their numbers went up again to 120,000. PSCAP ended unsuccessfully. Yet, the Zambian government felt that there was need for more and better reform. This is to be done by Zambia's present Public Sector Reform Programme (PSRP).

One question is what the optimum number of civil servants would be. The international auditors firm KPMG calculated that the optimum size for Zambia's civil service ranges between 80,000 and 99,000 depending on different (financial) scenarios. It is understandable that any government is under pressure to employ more civil servants. There is, so it seems, always a shortage of teachers and nurses. Hence, the demand is there, but governments' budget put a limit to the number of civil servants which it can afford.

Pay reform is one aspect of the PSRP. A pay reform study was started and should have been published some time ago. Such a study makes sense, as Zambia's remuneration system has perverse elements. The present sitting allowances, and the like, help improve one's income. Hence, they form attractive incentives to attend courses, seminars and overseas training, instead of attending to, for example, patients or to give classes. Obviously, pay reform should do away with perverse incentives. In some cases salary incentives are justified, such as providing better remuneration for school teachers and medical personnel posted in isolated areas of the country. However, performance monitoring and control mechanisms ought to accompany all this to ensure proper service delivery. The wage bill can also be controlled through a civil service census to establish the exact number of civil servants and to identify ghost workers (staff on government's pay roll who do not work there).

Any civil service requires capable senior managers, but good managers are hard to come by. Offering a select group of senior civil servants competitive salaries in order to attract and retain the best and brightest for the civil service is justified; it is applied in various highly successful (erstwhile) developing countries such as Singapore and South Korea, who both created an elite Senior Executive Service.

What is insufficiently done, I believe, is to make the civil service more efficient and effective with the same number -or even less- civil servants. Doing away with *red tape* is often a very simple and effective measure one can think of. Citizens can also help to make public service delivery more efficient by taking government to task. Providing vouchers to citizens in exchange of which they can get health or education services is another possibility. Decentralised service delivery can help to bring government and citizen's closer together. On top of that, outsourcing some activities, such as cleaning, security, transport and vehicle maintenance, cannot only help in keeping a tap on the number of civil servants, but may very well also help saving money for the treasury.

The other day I came across a description of a typical developing country public sector's context, which went as follows: 'The public sector provides conditions - present to varying degrees - in which government employees are unmotivated, ill-paid, and possibly absent from their jobs; where health clinics or other government offices may be locked up even though it is working hours; where government organisations do not listen to citizens and do not worry about or are not prepared to meet their needs, lack equipment and supplies, and lack adequately trained staff; where corruption is rife; where having to carry out business with a government office means endless red-tape, run-around, delays, and frustration; and where even the managers do not have up-to-date financial or other data to know how resources are being used and to what effect'. I am afraid that some of this rather dismal picture still applies to Zambia. The new President and his Cabinet have to rely on civil servants to implement the Government's policies. I am sure President Rupiah Banda and his ministers wish to demonstrate results. They can be best achieved through an efficient and effective civil service; that is why civil service reform, although not an exciting topic, is very important.

(2008)

Is Efficient Government Possible?

Is it possible that government institutions function efficiently? Can government be run along the lines of a business? These questions haunt many ministers and senior civil servants in poor countries, as ministries and other government institutions there are typically inefficient, ineffective and not very accountable to their clients: the taxpaying public.

I have always been convinced that government institutions in poor countries can function well, be it under certain conditions. I was lucky enough to test my conviction when I was working at the Netherlands Embassy in La Paz, Bolivia. There I had the opportunity to organize a study among five public institutions in Bolivia who appeared to work quite well. They were the Central Bank, the Bolivian Revenue Authority, the Customs Office, the National Fund for Rural Development and the Municipality of La Paz. Quite a mixed bag: some of them executed only administrative tasks such as the Revenue Authority and Customs. Others were mainly service delivery oriented, such as the Municipality of La Paz, and the Central Bank played its specific monetary role.

The study was set up along the following lines. Each of the five institutions provided one of their senior staff to collaborate in the study. They were asked to write an essay on the basis of a questionnaire which boiled down to the central question: What, according to you, are the factors explaining the efficient and successful functioning of your institution? The questionnaire was designed by the Public Administration Department of the Catholic University of La Paz, which had a close working relationship with Harvard's Kennedy School of Government, who joined the study as a back stopper.

During the time of the study, Bolivia's public sector was riddled with red-tape and (petty) corruption, low labour morale, poor service delivery, and staffed by civil servants, recruited not so much on the basis of their professional merits, but more on their loyalty to the political party in power. Hence, the five selected institutions were exceptions to the rule; they were, in other words, islands of excellence in an ocean of poor performance. How could that be; how was it possible that in the poorest country of South America, Bolivia, one could find institutions which functioned well?

The Catholic University researchers analysed the five essays written by the senior staff I just mentioned. Now, what conclusions did they draw from these five essays? Were their common success factors at play, or should the successful functioning of each institution be explained by specific factors, only applying to that particular institution? Interesting questions to which the researchers responded as follows.

From the outset they rightly stated that all of them enjoyed a certain degree of autonomy (such as hiring and firing of staff); yet, they also had to conform to certain general rules and constraints such as the dependence on budgets which were decided upon by others. They obviously also applied established rules and processes like any other bureaucracy.

The challenge for the five institutions was to create stability and a specific culture which would promote a sense of achievement and pride amongst staff. How was that done? A very important aspect was to prevent political interference in the vision and functioning of the institution at hand. Another one was the establishment of the specific mission of the institution concerned and to engrain that in the minds and actions of the staff, including a strong client orientation supported by the Internet, websites and call-centres. Corruption was not tolerated and the rule of complete transparency, internally as well as towards their clients, was strived for.

All this sounds logical, but how were all these crucial factors put into practice? A complicating factor all of the researched institutions were faced with (with the exception of the Central Bank) was that they had to overcome internal crises caused by political interference, incompetent personnel and/or corrupt practices. Regarding personnel, all four changed their entire staff and hired new staff based on professional qualifications. Their personnel policy also included career possibilities within the institution. It goes without saying that this radical measure was only possible with full political backing, which they had at the time, partly thanks to pressure from donors and partly thanks to an ongoing public sector reform programme.

The researchers touched upon a thorny issue regarding the management of large institutions, being the tension between the application of strict norms on the one hand and discretionary freedom on the other. This requires a bit of explanation. For example, immunization of children countrywide can be done in a uniform manner based on one clear set of instructions. However, attending patients in district health centres requires a degree of discretion so that the nurse or doctor can establish his or her own diagnosis and, based on that, take specific action. The same applies to education. The provision of text books can be done nationwide. But the relationship between teacher and pupil cannot be organised uniformly. The leaders of the institutions involved were able to maintain a balance between the application of the norm, but allowed discretion when required. Both, that is norms and discretion, should be adapted to the changing environment. If too rigid, the institution stands to lose its purpose or legitimacy. That is what the leaders also understood; organisational innovation was, therefore, another explanatory factor of efficient and successful functioning of their institutions.

Crucial in the entire process of the creation of well functioning public institutions was the pivotal role played by the leadership. They themselves directed the change for the better, based on their strong strategic thinking. They also created a sense of purpose and introduced a new organizational culture. What inspired them; what drove them? Was it an attractive salary or something beyond material remuneration? The researchers found that the salary aspect was not the main drive; their inspiration came much more from their ideas of what the role of their institution should be and their conviction that the institution could contribute to the well-being of the citizens. This may sound idealistic; yet, there is no doubt that these altruistic motives did play a very important role. Moreover, the leaders were gifted with excellent managerial skills. These skills are a rare commodity the world over. Hence, if they are available in a poor country, good managers can make a big difference.

What the leaders -supported by their senior managers- did, was to quickly set clear targets for the institution, communicate them to their staff and mould them into a workforce committed to achieve the targets. The researchers even wrote about a certain mystique which the leaders were able to instil into the workforce; meaning a sense of belonging to an institution which achieves something of which one can be proud, in other words: *esprit de corps.*

What the Bolivian experience tells us is that it is indeed possible to have government institutions function efficiently. And that is not because Bolivia is much better off than Zambia; no, it is almost equally poor. True, the institutions analysed all had a degree of independence which gave them the necessary breathing space to define their own personnel policy, their own operational standards, and -not in the least- they were isolated from political interference and crippling bureaucratic procedures.

The question is, would Bolivia's positive experience be applicable to Zambia? I would say, why not? There are legally established independent institutions here, such as the Office of the Auditor General, the Pharmaceutical Regulatory Authority, The National Aids Council, just to mention a few. If equipped with excellent managers, these (and other) institutions could be given the ways and means to strive for excellence in the public tasks they perform. This would not result in a better functioning of the entire public sector, but it certainly would result in better functioning public institutions, and in useful experiences which can be introduced in the public sector at large.

(2008)

Solutions When the Solution is The Problem

In the early days of foreign aid it was thought hat development could be planned. But development planning did not bring the results which were expected. Top development economists now say that we do not really know how to achieve development. Also in other development circles grandiose one size fits all-paradigms are making way for tailor-made approaches, fitting a particular country setting. The thinking now is that each aid receiving country has its own unique cultural, political, and economic environment within which development aid is to be designed and implemented.

William Easterly is a prominent representative of a new school of thought. In his successful book *The White Man's Burden*, Easterly writes that planning development has demonstrated to be a grandiose failure; instead we have to *search* for approaches that do work. Unfortunately, the question what search would work he did not answer. Just recently Easterly edited a new book: *Reinventing Foreign Aid*. Needless to say that I immediately rushed to a bookshop to buy it in the hope to find out what approach would work. Many well-known development thinkers contributed interesting essays, but the answer I was looking for was not provided. Yet, I was intrigued by some essays, and I would like to share the views some authors presented as they may contribute to the development debate in Zambia.

One essay sprang out, not only because of its funny title: *Solutions When the Solution Is the Problem*, but also because it demonstrates the dilemma development practitioners face in making real progress. The essay's authors, Pritchett and Woolcock, took delivery of public services, such as health and education, as their starting point. When there is failure to provide them properly, which is not uncommon in poor countries, donors typically send experts from rich country environments to design solutions for poor countries which are based on those of rich countries. Hence, these experts often provide remedies which do not work. The authors call this 'skipping straight to Weber', named after Max Weber who underscored the important role played by merit-based Western bureaucracies.

The proposed remedies are either of the intensification, amputation or policy reform type. Intensification means more of the same: if, for example, health services fail, the almost natural reaction is to provide more doctors and nurses. Amputation means that the service is taken away from government and is privatized, in the assumption that service delivery will improve. And policy reform means doing things differently. The authors present us a compelling picture of these remedies and their results, and demonstrate that often development advisors 'skip straight to Weber' in prescribing solutions. Most of them fail because, amongst others, the interactions of citizens, the state and service providers in the aid receiving country were simply overlooked. *The* solution was often presented as a logical approach to improvement of service delivery: *need* as the problem, *supply* as the solution, *civil service* as the instrument. True, this straightforward *common sense* approach has had successes, such as polio eradication and other immunization campaigns, but ended in far more failures, causing practitioners to doubt the usefulness of the *need-supply-civil service* way of fixing problems.

But what then? How do you go about service delivery problems if you can't apply logical and appealing solutions? There is a wide divide amongst scholars and practitioners on the question how to improve service delivery if *the* solution appears not to work. The essay tells us that effective service delivery depends on the structure of incentives facing providers and recipients. This structure happens to resemble the one identified in the *principal-agent* problem. The problem for the principal, whose objective, for example, is to provide health care and contracts an agent (his employee) to help achieve his objective but who may have a different objective (attending workshops to cash sitting allowances, for instance). Hence, the challenge is how to structure the incentives for the agent so that the agent's best interests, given the incentives involved, lead to efficient and effective health care.

The problem with the *needs-supply-civil service* solution was that it took as a starting point that all problems could be tackled through the logic of policies and programs. The needs-supply-civil service approach in education often led to schools with standardized curriculum, teachers with little training, low local commitment to the school, little real learning, and high drop-out rates. The failure can be explained by almost linear expectations, disregarding differences in incentives and a disregard for specific local circumstances. Evaluations of health programs typically revealed that some services were provided well (massive immunization for instance) and that some health conditions did improve, but often the services requiring individual curative attention did not. Clinics failed adequate staff, drugs and medical equipment. Is it a surprise then that patients did not even bother to go to government health facilities; they went straight to private clinics or traditional healers. Alas, these examples are rather reflective of Zambia's performance in education and health.

But the logic of *the* solution was so attractive to governments and donors alike that it has taken decades of painful and expensive failures in sector after sector to see that the problem was not just a few mistakes here and there, but that the solution was fundamentally wrong-headed from top to bottom. Why it took so long to discover that the solution was in fact the problem can be explained by the notion that as the solution worked in developed countries, so why not in developing ones? A second reason was that development aid was approached as an engineering problem whereby modern management techniques were applied. A third reason why the needs-supply-civil service solution is applied, especially by the poorest countries for such a long time, is that it fitted the interests of their donors, providing them with a powerful and convincing agenda for support. After all, nothing fits the internal needs of an aid agency better than an objectively quantifiable gap into which aid resources can be poured. As a result most aid receiving countries *'Skipped straight to Weber'*.

The essay confirms that there is a broad consensus that governments should be responsible for the provision of key public services: children should learn, roads should be passable, people should stay healthy. Okay, that does not surprise us. However, the big question is: *how* these services should be provided and they should ideally speaking be sustainable, accountable, responsive and transparent. It is quite a challenge to comply with all these conditions, let alone in adverse conditions in poor countries. Pritchett and Woolcock propose 7 different answers to this challenge: supplier autonomy, single-sector participation, contracting out, decentralisation, demand-side financing, social funds and community-driven development. They provide characteristics of each of them, such as where the financial resources come from, how information is organised, how decisions are being taken and by whom, and how delivery and accountability mechanisms work (the essay is unfortunately short on describing real life examples). Each of them can provide responses to failed past approaches of the need-supply-civil service kind. But are all of them right and universally applicable? Of course not; it depends on the specific environment in which they are to be applied. It is especially in the tension between the interests and incentives of administrators, clients, and frontline practitioners where the solutions lie. Hence, an open and flexible mind and attitude would be required to find appropriate approaches which lead to better service delivery. Both, government and the donors, have to play their part. As for the donors, they can help create the conditions under which genuine experiments and pilots can be undertaken to establish the most appropriate solutions for the improvement of service delivery.

(2008)

REVIEWS

The Bottom Billion by Paul Collier

Economic growth or no growth, that´s the question. Theories abound, but no one explains how growth is to be done. Hence, the quest for the right answer goes on. This review is about the latest attempt.

'The Third World has shrunk´, is the terrific first sentence of *The Bottom Billion*, Paul Collier`s latest book. He could have added another one: But the number of poor people has not changed over the past 20 years: it is still one billion; 70 % of them are Africans. Malawi at Independence was the poorest African country. Thirty five years later it is still as poor as it was then. In another 35 years it will not be much different, unless.... It is this "unless" that Collier`s book is about. What goes for Malawi also goes for Zambia.

Collier presents four traps that explain why the poorest countries did not catch up: the conflict trap, the natural resources trap, the landlocked and bad neighbours trap, and the bad governance trap. Not all of them apply to all countries, but one or more apply to all. Crucial in Collier´s propositions is that the problems of these bottom countries are very different from the ones which were addressed through aid so far. New forms of aid must be applied. But at the end of the day, it is the bottom countries to turn themselves around.

As for the traps, Zambia miraculously escaped the conflict trap; it is a haven of stability in the region. Hence, the trap of being poor triggering conflicts and civil war, which in turn promotes poverty, does not apply to Zambia. Civil war is development in *reverse*; it typically reduces growth by 2.3 % per year. Breaking the conflict trap is not a task that societies can accomplish by themselves, outside help is required. Collier pointed to the successful British intervention in Sierra Leone in 2001 as a case in point.

The natural resources trap applies to Zambia be it in a milder way than Angola, DRC, Sierra Leone, and Nigeria for example. Yet, Zambia did not transform gains from copper into diversification of its economy. The urge to do so was apparently not felt. But what about Botswana, dependent on diamond exports, registering the world´s fastest growth rate over a long period? Botswana combined a democratic development with effective checks and balances, plus productive public investments and a very large amount of surplus funds in foreign assets.

Zambia is landlocked. Almost 40 per cent of the bottom billion live in landlocked countries. But Switzerland, that little country, is also landlocked and yet it is one of the world's richest countries; how come? Switzerland, apart from having superior institutions, has excellent export transport links, while Zambia's links are poor. So being landlocked with poor transport links, it is very difficult to integrate into global markets for any product that requires a lot of transportation. Besides, Zambia is an expensive country with few skilled people and very low productivity and competitiveness. We know that it is precisely competition that promotes productivity growth. Zambia's intention to achieve a middle income status by 2030 is, given all these drawbacks, a far cry unless they are being countered urgently.

As for neighbours, countries benefit from their growth. If a country's neighbour grows by an additional 1 per cent, the country itself grows at an additional 0.4 percent, as Collier calculated. As for bad neighbours, Zimbabwe's economic meltdown is not very helpful to Zambia.

What can Zambia do? It can try not to be air-locked or E-locked. Another possibility is that it encourages remittances, which is already a significant source of income for many poor countries. Zambians living abroad should be encouraged to invest in Zambia, for example building homes for retirement, invest in businesses of their relatives, etc. It could also create a friendly environment for investment and resource exploration, promote rural development and attract more aid. The question then is how effective and with which urgency it will be done, as it is harder now than in the past to catch up.

What about the bad governance trap? It is not difficult to imagine that poor countries and poor governance coincide. Take Chad: less than 1 per cent of the monies meant for health clinics in Chad actually reached them, 99 per cent leaked away. It is hard to turn a bad governance situation around.

How aid can contribute

Can aid help to get the bottom billion countries out of stagnation and misery? Over the past 30 years aid has added 1 % to the annual growth rate of the bottom billion; but it should be noted that their overall growth rate was negative.

At the 2005 Gleneagles G-8 summit it was decided to double aid to Africa. Will this result in 2 % growth of poor countries? I don't think so. Lack of capacity and poor governance are the real bottlenecks. Moreover, aid happens to have diminishing returns, meaning that every extra aid dollar has less impact. Aid also has a Dutch disease effect, in that more aid monies result in the appreciation of the recipient country's currency, making their exports more expensive.

As for bad governance, aid can be helpful in creating incentives and improving skills. A recipient is rewarded with an aid premium for what it achieves. This is, for instance, how the USA's Millennium Challenge Account operates.

Then, skills. Bottom billion societies have lost whatever skills they once possessed, because the highly skilled now work in London, Washington or Paris. In these situations providing technical assistance (TA) to governments to e.g. strengthen their civil service makes sense. Because if the civil service is weak (being underpaid and moonlighting), whatever good policy will fail to be implemented. Aid by way of TA can fill that gap. As long as this TA is demand-driven and at the discretion of reform minded ministers it helps, concludes Collier.

Turning around a bottom billion failing state requires a *venture aid fund* model, operating on the principles of a venture capital fund, where taking risks implies potential losses, but huge gains as well. We, aid workers, are being evaluated -and promoted- on results achieved. Risk taking is thus averted, and one needs to take calculated risks in turnaround processes. This is what the British Government understood: they provided the World Bank with a fund to apply venture aid in turnaround situations.

Aid is often inspired by a sense of guilt: rich countries exploited poor ones; therefore they have to make up by giving them aid. I share Collier's view that the rich world is not to blame for most of the bottom billion's problems; poverty is mainly a consequence of malfunctioning economies. That prompts the question: what should be done? As the Asian Tigers have shown diversify the economy into labour intensive manufactures and services, and export. The problem for the bottom billion is that they come late to this game because the Asians are far more competitive. Collier proposes to *pump-prime* African exports by offering them preferential tariffs. What this means is that goods and services exported from the bottom billion to rich world markets would pay lower tariffs than the same goods coming from Asia.

The Bottom Billion is a passionate book. It is addressed to all of us, because all of us can help overcome the bottom billions bleak plight. Voters in rich countries can take their Governments to task regarding ineffective aid and protective tariff walls. Their political leaders can take bold measures in favour of poor countries´ rapid development. Aid agencies can apply Collier's suggestions and focus their efforts more on bottom billion societies. Finally, and not in the least, bottom billion Governments should understand the urgency of their situation and take brave steps to break free from poverty and stagnation, and move forward on the road to growth and prosperity.

(2007)

Culture Matters; Ed: Lawrence E. Harrison and Samuel P. Huntington

Culture matters: that is what sociologists and anthropologists say when talking about development. But historians say that history matters. And economists used to say that economics matter; that is, until a couple of decades ago when they found that their growth theories did not match what happened in real life. How come? What is it that triggers economic growth?

Harvard's Michael Porter presented us with a typical growth path: Economic progress is a process of successive upgrading, in which a nation's business environment evolves to support increasingly sophisticated and productive ways of competing. As regards the process of growth, for a country to move out of poverty (Zambia for example), it must upgrade its inputs, institutions, and skills to allow more sophisticated forms of competition, resulting in increased productivity. This requires upgrading its human capital, improving infrastructure, opening trade and foreign investment, protecting intellectual property, improving product quality and environmental impact, and expanding regional integration. This is Porter's recipe, but how a ´growth brew´ is being prepared is quite another matter.

In dealing with this 'how' question, culture came in. A formidable representative of the cultural dimension of growth was Max Weber, whose *The Protestant Ethic and the Spirit of Capitalism* of 1905, is still often quoted, wherein Weber explained the rise of capitalism as a cultural phenomenon rooted in the protestant religion. Recently, economists entered the domain of culture after they concluded that the neo-classical growth model was incapable of explaining growth or the lack of it. The neo-classicists ignored the *incentives structure* of societies, which explains why so many economies stagnate and why sustained growth is so difficult to achieve. The incentive structure of a society is moulded by its particular culture and history. It is this type of thinking that made some economists enter into the uncharted territory of culture, despite the fact that many mainstream economists were convinced that appropriate economic policy, effectively implemented, would produce the same results, irrespective culture!

Yet, this small band of dissenting economists has not been shy to apply economics to aspects of social behaviour, including game theory. This was not done without difficulties, as terms like 'social behaviour' and 'culture' are difficult to define and equally difficult to integrate in econometric growth models. Yet, attempts have been made by prominent economists, sociologists, and historians and were brought together in an interesting collection of essays under the title (indeed!) *Culture Matters*.

Therein, a Cameroonian scholar, Daniel Etounga-Manguelle, deals with the cultural obstacles hindering Africa's growth. He says that traditional cultural values are at the root of poverty, authoritarianism, and injustice in Africa. True, this is a sweeping statement; but without bold statements culture's role in development can not clearly shine through. After all, it is hard to precisely characterise African culture; there are many sub-cultures. But Etounga believes that it makes sense to generalise about African culture, because there is a foundation of shared values, attitudes, and institutions that binds together the nations south of the Sahara.

Etounga tried to capture what he thought would be the *essential hindering elements* to growth, most of them the reader will probably recognise. Hierarchical distance is such an element, he says. In societies with substantial hierarchical distance, such as in Africa, the society tends to be static and politically centralised. The generations pass without significant change in mind-set. The lack of control over uncertainty would be another element. Etounga says that African societies condition their members to accept uncertainty about the future, taking each day as it comes. Nature is his master and sets his destiny.

Then, there is the tyranny of time. A Nigerian saying is 'A watch did not invent man', reflective of Africans having their own concept of time. That may have its advantages, in that one lives according to its own rhythm. However, the downside of it is that quite a lot of other societies value time, have a sense of urgency, are disciplined, and successfully take part in the globalised world, reaping the rewards that come from it.

Etounga further notes that in Africa the community dominates the individual. The African can only develop and bloom in social and family life, Etounga notes. Something the Africans have in common with Latinos is that they have a propensity to feast. Everything, from birth to marriage and even death, is a pretext for celebration. Saving for the future has a lower priority than consumption, suggests Etounga.

Moreover, those who have a regular income have to finance the studies of brothers, cousins; you name it, and finance the multitude of ceremonies that fill social life. Then, there is witchcraft, widely practiced still in Africa; the opposite of rationalism. And it is rationalism that is crucial in confronting the challenges of economic growth.

At the end of his sobering overview, Etounga yet passionately concludes that Africans must keep their humanistic values, such as high degrees of warmth, solidarity and reciprocity, but they must overcome the obstacles to economic progress and social well-being.

Not all authors of *Culture Matters* are convinced that culture is an important explanatory factor of growth. One dissenter is Jeffrey Sachs who tries to demonstrate that culture is an insignificant factor compared to the influence of geography and climate. Sachs reminds us that the temperate regions of the world are vastly more developed than the tropics. Prosperous Hong Kong and Singapore are exceptions. Sachs also notes that not all temperate-zone regions have done well: North Africa and parts of the Southern Hemisphere (Argentina, Chile, Uruguay, South Africa); all of them are lagging behind, thereby in fact confirming that the available growth theories may apply to some countries, but there are always exceptions which don't fit.

Sachs applies an econometric model to test the influence of culture on economic development. As for the counties in the temperate zones, North Africa and the Middle East underperformed. So did Argentina, Uruguay and South Africa. Would the cultural dimension explain this? Sachs concludes that it is impossible to isolate the cultural dimension from others, such as opposition to market-based institutions or trade discrimination from Europe. Argentina and Uruguay are populated by European immigrants; why then would they lag behind? In fact, both were doing better before World War II than most of Europe; hence, their poor performance after the war must be explained by counterproductive domestic economic policies. South Africa's under-performance must be explained by apartheid and colonial policies.

What about successful tropical countries? Only Singapore and Hong Kong (both very small) stand out. Runners up are Botswana, Mauritius, Gabon, Colombia, Costa Rica, Thailand and Trinidad & Tobago. Does culture explain their economic success? Malaysia and Thailand's success could well be explained by the strong role played by its large Chinese entrepreneurial community. All told, Sachs concludes that culture plays a subsidiary role to the broader geographical and political/economic dimensions.

I believe that Sachs is downplaying the role of culture in the development of the successful temperate zone countries. After all, the large majority of them have a protestant background, which, according to Max Weber, is *the* driving force of progress. Sachs confirms that there is justification in explaining the phenomenal growth of East Asian countries thanks to their respective Chinese entrepreneurial communities. Would not have the deeply rooted Confucian culture have played its role there?

Africa is a late comer in development. Whether it will be able to catch up depends on many factors. After all, growth and development cannot be explained by one overriding factor only. But I believe that its cultural characteristics explain to some extent that Africa has not taken off yet. As for Zambia, it has a lot of potential to achieve its ambition of becoming a middle income by 2030. If the proceeds from the present growth will be invested in improving infrastructure, energy supply and in the capabilities of its human resources, Zambia might really take off!

(2008)

False Economy by Alan Beattie

What makes some countries prosper and others not? Another intriguing question is what happened to economic top performers who have fallen on hard times? Could one overarching growth theory explain the broad spectrum of economic growth and stagnation which the world has witnessed during the past two millennia? From time to time economists thought they had the answer; unfortunately, their growth theories were all proven wrong when it turned out that not all economies responded equally. That is the trouble for development economists: for any growth model there are economies which don't conform.

I came across a nice book which takes a crack at these questions. *False Economy* is its title, authored by Alan Beattie, a Financial Times world trade editor. Beattie starts his book by comparing Argentina and the United States of America. At the beginning of the last century Argentina was one of the world's richest countries, it went bust in 2001, and it is now at best a modest middle income country. In contrast, the USA is the mightiest economy in the world. So what went wrong with Argentina, given the fact that it enjoyed comparable economic opportunities to those of the USA? A mix of the wrong economic policies inspired by the wrong pressure groups explains Argentina's downfall. *False Economy's* central theme is that countries make choices that determine the path their economies take.

Argentina and the USA were agricultural countries pushing their settlements westward by gauchos and cowboys, so to speak. But America chose a path that parcelled out new land to individuals; Argentina delivered the land into the hands of a few rich landowners. Both countries benefitted from the first wave of globalisation (1880-1914). By the end of the 19th century income per head in Argentina was higher than that of France.

Argentina's landowners spent their proceeds from agricultural exports in imported consumer goods, whilst America *invested* the gains in industrialization. The saying at the time was: the New World did farming and Europe did machines. The elites of Argentina rejected the mentality that industrialisation required not spending one's gains but investing them in industrialisation. Argentina's development depended on their farm export prices to hold their own against the prices of manufactured goods, and on the global markets remaining open.

In hindsight, the defining moment for America's growth was the Civil War in which the industrialised North defeated the agrarian South. Argentina remained stuck in the old ways; economically it had a single world-class agricultural sector dependent on demand from abroad and on imported capital and technology. By the end of the First World War American industry had become the best in the world. Then came the Depression of the 1930s. President Roosevelt acted correctly through his *New Deal* stimulus package. Argentina was paralysed by the economic crisis. Their beef exports dropped dramatically while the country was already deep in debt. Dictatorship ensued and in 1946 Juan Peron took the helm. Argentina's thinking was that relying on outside markets and on foreign capital was a mistake, so Argentina became looking inwards. Argentina adopted an *import substitution policy that* is industrialisation cut off from the outside world, behind a high wall of tariff protection.

The veteran development economist, Simon Kuznets, retorted at the time: there are four types of countries developed and developing countries, Japan and Argentina; of course referring to the phenomenal growth of Japan and Argentina's embarrassing decline. Argentina ran into persistent balance of payment problems, running inflation, and eventually it defaulted in 2001.

Both America and Argentina were hit by the recent financial crisis. Argentina reacted by appropriating the country's private pension funds; that is seizing its peoples savings to counter the loss of investor's confidence. The US government has invested heavily in bailing out banks, insurance companies, the ailing carmakers, and is propping up the financial regulatory system which had miserably failed. Beattie concluded that it was history and choice and *not* fate which determined why the USA is still the world's leading economy and why Argentina declined.

Beattie deals with the role played by trade, corruption and the natural resource curse. He compares the diverging development paths followed by diamond rich Sierra Leone (which is in a mess) and Botswana (which is the world's best grower during the past 4 decades). Also Zambia's persistent dependence on copper is extensively dealt with.

Particularly interesting I found the way he deals with the role of religion in development. Being a believer in Max Weber's thinking that Protestantism promotes growth, I was taken by surprise. Let me explain. Beattie refutes the conventional wisdom that Islam has a negative influence on economic growth. That is nonsense, he says, as there are quite a few Islamic countries which have grown, and sustainably so. Malaysia is one of them and so is Indonesia (home to the largest number of Muslims). Beattie conveniently forgets to mention that both countries do benefit substantially from Chinese entrepreneurship! He rightly says that growth or stagnation has more to do with the actions of priests, politicians, monarchs and bureaucrats exploiting religious doctrine to pursue wealth and power. As for political dynamics involved in economic development, it was that European merchants were powerful enough to have inconvenient laws disposed of, even when that required changing the religious justification of those laws. Their counterparts in Islamic countries, for reasons largely unrelated to the nature of religion itself, were not. Even Max Weber accepted later in life that while the Protestant ethic had helped get modern capitalism going; it now had momentum of its own and could be adopted by any society!

As for trade, *False Economy* laments about the deadlock in the Doha Round; the international negotiations to lower tariffs to free up international trade. However, the author states that the benefits for developing countries would have been limited anyway, as the biggest impediment to trade for them lies in their own poor infrastructure and the difficulties posed in doing business. For example, the West African cotton growing countries were right to press the US to reduce their cotton subsidies. But the best way of making farmers in countries like Mali better off would be to upgrade the supply chain; i.e. improving the state marketing board, which currently pays farmers less than 50 per cent of the world price for their produce, and building a viable spinning and weaving industry rather than exporting raw cotton.

Beattie concludes that economic stagnation is to a large extent caused by influential groups or 'elites' who have a stake in maintaining the *status-quo*. Argentina's trajectory is a case in point. The question then is, and a highly relevant one for stagnant poor countries like Zambia: can they turn themselves around quickly? *Yes, they can*, argues Beattie, if they apply the right policies. China's and India's phenomenal growth during the past few decades comes to mind. Both countries were basically stagnant and inward looking until Deng Xiao Ping opened the Chinese economy up in 1979. And in 1991, then finance Minister Manmohan Singh managed to open up the Indian economy to overcome its serious signs of economic sclerosis.

All in all, *False Economy* is a spicy and thought provoking book. Having taken the reader through the various successful and failed growth attempts, Beattie admits that he doesn't know the exact answers. What he says is that a few basic ideas are now accepted. A major one is not to isolate a county from the rest of the world. And let an economy do what it is best at. Watch for elites who are only after maintaining the status-quo; that certainly will hinder any sort of development. Respect property rights and the rule of law. And a final warning: globalisation increases the potential rewards for countries that can get their policies right but makes more obvious the gaps between them and those that cannot.

(2009)

Philanthro-Capitalism by Matthew Bishop and Michael Green

Sometimes I ask friends what they would do if they were to win the jackpot of, say, $15 million. Invariably they respond that they would buy a nice house for themselves, their brothers, sisters and parents. What else, I ask? A long silence ensues, as they really don't know off hand what to spend the rest of their fortune on. Some contemplate charity, others would invest in the arts; the least entrepreneurial would simply put it into a savings account.

Well, what is difficult for us -poor souls- is equally difficult for super rich philanthropists. Warren Buffett, who -as you know- donated his fortune to the Bill and Melinda Gates Foundation, once said that giving away money is a tougher game than making it. Philanthropy has gotten a tremendous boost since the world's two richest men, Bill Gates and Warren Buffett, gave away a very large part of their wealth. The Gates Foundation has assets worth $33.1 billion. Buffett added $37 billion, making the foundation by far the world's largest charitable foundation.

Philanthropy is as old as the world. Philanthropy is not exclusively an American or Western phenomenon. Indian King Ashoka, for example, is remembered as a benevolent ruler. Islamic law specifically includes *zakat*, alms giving. The Aga Khan Foundation is doing very commendable work in many parts of the world. The Mo Ibrahim Prize and the Nelson Mandela Foundation are two African philanthropic initiatives.

Modern problem-solving philanthropy was invented way back during the Tudor era in Great Britain in tandem with the emergence of capitalism. Economic growth during the past two decades triggered a spurt in philanthropy. This was preceded by earlier cycles of philanthropy, i.e. during the Victorian era in Britain, followed by another wave in the United States led by famous philanthropists such as steel magnate Andrew Carnegie and oil tycoon David Rockefeller, who established the Rockefeller Foundation. Car maker Henry Ford followed suit by creating the Ford Foundation.

What makes rich people turn to philanthropy, and are philanthropists more successful in 'doing good' than traditional donor agencies? With these intriguing questions in mind I started to read *Philanthro-Capitalism*, by Matthew Bishop and Michael Green.

What made Bill Gates, Warren Buffett, and Michael Bloomberg (just to mention a few) give away their capital? They are Americans, and being generous with one's wealth forms part of the American culture. They may very well have been inspired by the illustrious Andrew Carnegie who wrote an essay called *Wealth*. In fact it was Warren Buffett who gave Gates a copy of this essay. Carnegie felt hat the rich should dispose of their wealth *during their lifetime*, so that: 'the ties of brotherhood may still bind together the rich and poor in harmonious relationship', in Carnegie's own words. He saw philanthropy as an answer to the social problems created by a spurt in wealth creation. 'The rich', he argued, 'have it in their power during their lives to busy themselves in organising benefactions from which the masses of their fellows will derive lasting advantage'. And that is precisely what Bill Gates and the like are doing as social entrepreneurs. A specific second reason for Gates to turn to philanthropy was provided by a World Bank report on investing in health in poor countries. After reading it Gates said that a life in Africa is worth no less than a life in America, and that he had an opportunity to use his enormous wealth to correct the injustice. The sage from Omaha, Warren Buffett, certainly will have had similar ideas as Gates. Both went public; everybody knows that the two richest men join forces for the good. There are other super-rich people who give away tons of money on the strict condition of anonymity. The owner of Duty Free shops at airports, Chuck Feeney, is one of them. Only long after he had donated billions of dollars to causes ranging from health care, improving the quality of education in Ireland to funding part of the peace process there, it became known that he funded these initiatives. Studies have been done to map the range of motives that trigger philanthropy. Guilt feeling is one; another one is the sheer pleasure of giving and the status and admiration that goes with it. Yet another reason is to further the interests of the core activities of the philanthropist, be it business, the arts, etc. However, pure altruism can only be achieved according to the French philosopher Jacques Derrida when the giver never knows that he has given a gift and the recipient never knows that he has received it. Well, that seems to me a bit too pure.

Since the very rich have the talent to make a lot of money -which most of us don't- the assumption seems justified that when they apply it to doing good, they do it very well. The philanthropist can do whatever he likes; he is not constrained by political motives and he can take risks and doesn't have to render account but -strictly speaking-to himself!

One of the main themes of *Philanthro-capitalism* is philanthropy applied with a clear purpose and delivered in a business-like manner. The book reveals that philanthropists have not only achieved success and impact. Take the Ford Foundation for example. It gives out 2,000 grants every year of $50,000 - on average. One critic asked how many social problems can be solved with $50,000.-? Not many, and with little lasting impact. Shell Foundation's director, Kurt Hoffman, made a scathing comment about the traditional donor community and philanthropic foundations: 'The international development community, donors, NGOs and foundations created by rich people are stuffed full of issue experts who don't know how to solve problems or produce scalable solutions'. But, what does Shell Foundation offer instead? Shell Foundation, explains Hoffman, created an investment fund for small- and medium African enterprises that cannot get funding elsewhere. This is nothing new; others have successfully done so before. The difference is the *leveraging* dimension in Shell Foundation's approach. It put up $12 million of its own capital and through that levered $100 million of commercial investments last year. It expects to soon attract up to $250 million, thereby creating many jobs and promoting growth in Africa. Hoffman claims that the Foundation's early success is due to its access to the expertise its parent company (Shell Oil) has in finance, marketing, logistics, etc.

Leveraging is an important strategic tool of the modern philanthropist. Take billionaire and New York's mayor, Michael Bloomberg. He piloted education improvement experiments in New York schools with his own money (and Gates' by the way) before having successful pilots hugely scaled up through government funds. Bloomberg also donated $125 million for research in stopping smoking. After he became New York's mayor he had a small law passed to ban smoking in New York's public places which had an immediate and far reaching impact, as his example was soon taken over by neighbouring States and then Europe. Even Bill Gates is fully aware that without leveraging, his support will be a drop in the ocean. The Gates

Foundation spent $1.5 billion in 2006. A large part of it went into research and the fight against AIDS, malaria and TB. However, if this amount would not have been greatly topped up by donors such as the Global Fund and PEPFAR, Gates would not be able to make a difference. The challenges at hand in the killer diseases are simply too big, even for Bill Gates.

The great value of modern philanthropy is its ability to put large amounts of money on the table, be innovative, tap the best minds to confront problems, and show eagerness to lever their support with that of the traditional donors, of which large parts of the developing world, including Zambia, is benefitting.

(2009)

A Farewell to Alms by Gregory Clark

A few months ago I visited the Centre for Global Development, a think tank in Washington DC. I felt humbled by the scholars there. All were sitting behind their computer screens and they were thinking. They did not say much; now and again they uttered a deep sigh. They wrote mighty articles and some of them were even busying themselves writing books! Since they were silent, I took the opportunity to inspect their libraries; not large ones, but to the point. In one of them I spotted *A farewell to Alms,* by Gregory Clark.

Now, that was a creative title! It was clearly based on Hemingway's *A farewell to Arms,* inspired by his experience as an ambulance driver during the Great War. Clark's book, however, is about the history of the world's economic development; not a small subject to tackle! Yet in his introductory chapter Clark wrote that the basic outline of world economic history is surprisingly simple.

The history is as follows: until the year 1800 the world didn't develop much, economically speaking. But after the *Industrial Revolution* in Great Britain, the world witnessed phenomenal economic growth. But that didn't apply to all countries. What happened since then is a widening gap between the countries which followed Britain's example, and those which lagged behind. Clark calls this widening gap the *Great Divergence.* What is interesting about Clark's book is not so much this historic overview; it is his interpretation of events.

Now, let us take a look at the period before the Industrial Revolution. Clark concludes that before 1800 income per person, i.e. the food, clothing, and housing available per person, varied across societies and periods. But there was no upward trend! There was a simple mechanism behind this: the Malthusian Trap, named after Thomas Malthus (1766-1834) who predicted that population growth would outgrow the (agricultural) production capacity of a society. The crucial factor is the very slow rate of technological advance, which explains why material conditions could not permanently improve. Moreover, any improvement in technology, triggering higher production, resulted in population growth which -in turn- put too much pressure on the limited food production. Hence, the population's well being and their numbers were oscillating around an equilibrium, explaining the fact that the average person in 1800 was no better off than the average person say 100,000 years ago.

The quality of life also did not change much during the entire period before 1800. For example, life expectancy was no higher in 1800 than for hunter-gatherers thousands of years before. Nor did the variety of material consumption improve. The average forager had a diet and a work life much more varied than the typical English worker of 1800, even though the English diet then included luxuries such as tea, pepper and sugar. Clark concludes (based on a lot of statistical analyses) that the average welfare declined from the Stone Age to 1800.

The Malthusian era was shattered by two big events: the Industrial Revolution, i.e. the appearance for the first time of rapid economic growth fuelled by increasing production efficiency, made possible by advances in technology. The other big event was a decline in fertility which started with the upper class and gradually included all society. Income per person began to grow in a small group of countries.

Were some countries economically speaking successful, others, mainly in Sub-Saharan Africa, were left out. These African countries, including Zambia, remained trapped in the Malthusian era, where technological advances (such as in medicine) merely produced more people and consequently living standards were driven down to the subsistence level. Just as the Industrial Revolution reduced income inequalities within societies, it has increased them between societies leading to the Great Divergence.

These historical developments beg the following three questions; why did the Malthusian trap persist for so long, i.e. hundreds of thousands of years? Question number two is: why did the initial escape from that trap occur in England around 1800? And number three: why was there a divergence afterwards, and didn't all societies follow suit?

Clark maintains that the Industrial Revolution did not happen all of a sudden; a long gestation period preceded it. Let me explain. He says that the economic laws governing human society were subject to Darwinian natural selection throughout the Malthusian era. This Darwinian struggle didn't end with the Neolithic Revolution (when settled agricultural societies appeared) but continued right up until the Industrial Revolution. Clark demonstrates this by comparing economic successful people in England during the six centuries preceding the Industrial Revolution. Economic success translated into reproductive success. In other words, the richest men had twice as many surviving children at death as the poorest. The attributes that ensure economic dynamism, such as patience, hard work, ingenuity, education, innovativeness, were thus spreading biologically throughout the population. This sounds plausible; nonetheless Clark's observation implies a politically incorrect statement, namely that economic dynamism would be explained by a natural selection process based on the survival of the economically fittest.

This selection process was accompanied by changes in the characteristics of the preindustrial economy, due largely to the population's adoption of more middle class preferences. Interest rates fell, murder rates declined, work hours increased, and numeracy and literacy spread even to the lower reaches of society. Clark concludes that the centuries before the Industrial Revolution had profoundly shaped the culture, and may be even the *genes*, of the members of agrarian societies. It was these slow and incremental changes that eventually created the possibility of an Industrial Revolution only around 1800.

But why did the Industrial Revolution start in England and not for example in China, India or Japan? Clark answers as follows. The extraordinary stability of England back at least to 1200, the slow growth of the English population between 1300 and 1760, and the extraordinary fertility of the rich and economically successful, explain why England had created the most conducive environment around 1800. The embedding of bourgeois values into the culture, and perhaps even the genetics, was for these reasons the most advanced in England, Clark added. China and Japan both moved into the same direction as England between 1600 an 1800 but the Chinese and Japanese upper strata of society procreated less than their English counterparts.

The Industrial Revolution has had profound social effects. As a result of two forces, i.e. the nature of technological advance and the demographic transition, economic growth in capitalist economies since the Industrial Revolution strongly promoted equality. The unskilled benefitted most from this economic revolution, despite the *conventional wisdom* that the capitalists would have been the big winners!

Now, what is most important for Zamia and other poor African countries is the question why the Great Divergence happened. Clark demonstrated that the Industrial Revolution widened the gap between rich and poor countries. The reason for this is diverging productivity: modern production technologies developed in rich countries are designed for labour forces that are disciplined, conscientious, and engaged. When workers in poor countries lack these qualities of discipline and engagement, productivity remains very low and competitiveness is lost.

Clark provides new -and daring- insights in the historical course of economic development. He criticizes the popular opinion that it is institutions which explain growth. Clark noted that England, but also China and India, did avail of the right institutions already long ago, and yet these institutions didn't trigger development. Clark points at the long gestation period for rich countries' economic *take off*, amongst others helped by genetic processes in those countries. The question then arises: why is it that immigrants from poor countries into rich ones do often adapt and turn out to be successful in economic terms? It may be that successful immigrants have the talent and attitude to get ahead in life, but couldn't do so in their home countries because of political and institutional hindrances there. All in all, Clark has opened our mind to other dimensions in the unending quest for growth, but they may not be the only ones.

(2009)

Empire by Niall Ferguson

Did Britain make the modern world? This intriguing question formed the central theme of Niall Ferguson's book *Empire*. Ferguson is a British historian of Scottish stock who took on the formidable task to write a history of the British Empire while trying to answer two questions. The first one was how an archipelago of rainy islands off the north-west coast of Europe came to rule the world? The second -and more difficult one- was simply whether the Empire was a good or bad thing? And it is about the latter question that this essay is about.

As there are no objective criteria to pass a verdict on the merits of the British Empire, Ferguson takes a few (he calls them features) to measure Britain's performance as a colonizer. True, this is debatable; yet, it is a fascinating endeavour. In fact, the opinions of the British themselves changed over time, and there were quite wide differences between them. To illustrate: I once saw a very good documentary done by Simon Schama (another formidable British historian) on the varying opinions. Schama pitted Winston Churchill, a staunch defender of the Empire, against George Orwell, a strong opponent. When Orwell served as a colonial officer in Burma he wrote one of his best short stories about him having to kill an elephant who had run amok. Orwell wrote: 'In the end the sneering yellow faces of young men that met me everywhere, the insults hooted after me when I was at a safe distance , got badly on my nerves... For at the time I had already made up my mind that Imperialism was an evil thing and the sooner I chucked up my job and got out the better'. Yet, he concluded: 'I did not even know that the British Empire is dying, still less did I know that it is a great deal better than the younger empires that are going to supplant it'. I believe Orwell had the Soviet Empire in mind.

Churchill was a staunch defender of the British Empire from a very young age on. He once told a fellow Harrowian, when Winston was only 17 years old: 'I can see vast changes coming over a peaceful world; great upheavals, terrible struggles; wars such as one cannot imagine; and I tell you London will be in danger, London will be attacked and I shall be prominent in the defence of London...and I shall save London and the Empire from disaster'.

Ferguson doubts whether the world would have been the same, or even similar, in the absence of the Empire. Even if one were to allow for the possibility that trade, capital flows and migration could have been 'naturally occurring' in the past 300 years, there remains the flow of British culture and institutions. When the British governed a country there were certain distinctive features of their own society that the British disseminated. Ferguson provides a list of 9 of these features: the English language, English forms of land tenure, English banking, the Common law, Protestantism, team sports, the limited 'night watchman' state, representative assemblies, and the idea of liberty. He adds that the idea of liberty remains the most distinctive feature of the Empire which sets it apart from its continental rivals. I would not be surprised if the French would strongly disagree. After all, the motto of the French revolution was: Liberty, equality, fraternity.

What Ferguson demonstrates in his book, while taking the reader through the breathtaking history of the Empire, is that whenever the British were behaving despotically (which they did in various well-known instances) there was almost always a liberal critique of that behaviour from *within* British society. So, once a colonized society had sufficiently adopted the other British institutions, it became very hard for the British to prohibit that political liberty aspired by the colonized. Ferguson illustrates this with the independence struggle of the United States, India and -not to overlook-Ireland; by the way, the first country to have been colonized: Henry VIII proclaimed himself as King of Ireland in 1541. Yet the Empire -the largest the world has ever known- spanned more than 300 years and had a far larger 'imprint' than other Empires. Ferguson asks: 'In dilapidated Chinsura (India), a vision of how all Asia might look if the Dutch Empire had not declined and fallen. Would New Amsterdam be the New York we know today if the Dutch had not surrendered it to the British in 1664? I note though that the Brits took over a lot of useful things from the Dutch which helped them overtake them as empire builders. The American historian Russell Shorto recently concluded that the Dutch introduced liberal thinking in New Amsterdam, which influenced the spirit of the Declaration of Independence.

The early inspiration for empire building was purely economic: the demand for sugar from the Caribbean and spices and textiles from the Far East, and the slave trade. Much later states were formed and British designed institutions were introduced, including in Zambia. Popular thinking has it that the Empire went rapidly under after the Second World War was a result of popular uprisings in the colonies, notably in India. Ferguson disagrees. Britain couldn't any longer afford its colonies; not only because they had become net spenders, but especially because Britain was exhausted and financially *down and out* as a result of the huge costs of two terrible wars: the Great War and the Second World War, and the Economic Depression in between. The great creditor had become a debtor.

Now, back to the central question: was the Empire a good or bad thing? Ferguson compares the British Empire with the Russian alternative, who imposed incalculable misery on their subjects. And he goes on: without the influence of the British imperial rule, it is hard to believe that the institutions of parliamentary democracy would have been adopted by the majority of the states in the world. Take India, the world's largest democracy. Its elite schools, its universities, its civil service, its army, its press and parliamentary system all still have discernibly British models. I would retort that where British settled in relatively large numbers, such as in South Africa and Rhodesia, they did not mix with the local population, took the best lands and controlled other economic activities. The result was a strongly divided society. There is, of course, the English language, perhaps Britain's most important single export over the past 300 years. Today close to 400 million people speak English as their first language and around 500 million have it as a second language, including myself.

The Empire paved the way for economic globalization and certainly benefitted from it, like others, during the first globalization wave around the turn of the 19th century. Ferguson underscores this point by noting that by relinquishing Britain's colonies in the second half of the 19th century would probably have led to higher tariffs in their markets, and perhaps other forms of trade discrimination. The evidence for this is that it manifested itself in the huge protectionist policies adopted by the United States and India after they secured independence. True at the time, but a shaky piece of evidence, I'd say. Another positive effect of the Empire was the promotion of migration;

again true but for economic reasons benefitting the Empire. Take the large quantities of Indian indentured labourers who toiled on far-flung plantations in the Caribbean, the Far East, Africa, and the Pacific. They often suffered but their plight at home was not much better and their offspring had better economic prospects than in their home country.

Ferguson also points to the fact that the British Empire facilitated the export of capital to the less developed world. In 1996 only 28 % of foreign direct investment went to developing countries, whereas in 1913 the proportion was 63 %. A plausible hypothesis is that the Empire encouraged investors to put their money in developing economies, as the risk involved was perceived as less given British rule there.

Those opposing imperialism maintain that the British Empire impoverished their colonies. Ferguson responds that it can't be denied that many former colonies are still exceedingly poor. Today, for example, per capita GDP in Britain is roughly 28 times Zambia's. But to blame this on the legacy of colonialism is not very persuasive, when the differential between Britain and Zambian incomes was so much less at the end of the colonial period. In 1955, for example, British per capita GDP was just 7 times greater than Zambia's. Since Zambia's independence in 1964 the gap between the colonizer and the ex-colony has dramatically widened. Ferguson confirms that the same is true for nearly all former colonies in Sub-Saharan Africa, with the notable exception of Botswana. This does in fact undermine Ferguson's idea that the British were doing a better job than other colonizers. If Africa were to be judged along those lines, I am afraid that the British did not do better than e.g. the French.

Ferguson continues by stating that in successful former colonies (e.g. the USA, Canada, Australia, New Zealand) it was British-style institutions, such as British law and lean administration, that tended to enhance a country's economic prospects. This is no surprise, as the British settlers completely marginalized the local populations in those former colonies.

Ferguson got support from another formidable economic historian, the American David Landes. He drew up an interesting list of measures which the *'ideal growth-and-development'* government would adopt: (1)

87

secure rights of private property; (2) secure rights to private liberty; (3) enforce rights of contracts: (4) provide stable government; (5) provide responsive and honest government; (6)provide moderate, efficient, ungreedy government.

Ferguson concludes by saying that the striking thing about this list is how many of its points correspond to what British Indian and Colonial officials in the 19th and 20th century believed they were doing, inspired by the so-called *ethical policy*. Yet, the British argument for postponing the transfer to democracy was that many of their colonies were not ready for it; indeed, the classic 20th century line from the Colonial Office was hat Britain's role was precisely to get them ready. This rather paternalistic view was equally shared by the Dutch regarding Indonesia's independence. My question is then: why didn't the colonizers prepare the local populations much earlier for independence? A case in point is Zambia: at independence only approximately100 Zambians had completed university education. By the way, Indonesia's record was not much better when it achieved independence from the Dutch.

The trouble with history and other social sciences is that there are no objective standards, such as in physics and chemistry, to test Ferguson's very interesting hypothesis on the Empire. I believe that Britain's contribution to a globalized world is undeniable; regarding the other claims apart from English as the world's *lingua franca*, there is less basis for a positive verdict. As Sir Richard Turnball, the former Governor of Aden, told Labour politician Dennis Healey: 'When the British Empire finally sank, it left behind only two monuments: one was the game of Association Football, the other is the expression 'Fuck off''.

(2009)

Dead Aid by Dambisa Moyo

The other day I passed by a bookshop in town and saw in the middle of the shop window a book with a striking title: *Dead Aid*. Its subtitle was: Why Aid is not working and how there is another way for Africa. As I am working in the domain of development aid, I wrote this review with a donor's perspective in mind. *Dead Aid* is written by Dambisa Moyo, a Zambian lady. Ms. Moyo has an impressive curriculum which includes a PhD in Economics at Oxford University. She also has wide experience in the financial world as Head of Economic Research and Strategy for Sub-Saharan Africa at Goldman Sachs.

Zambians can be proud of her as her book is well written and it is a *bomb shell* of a book. Why is that? Because Ms. Moyo is angry about the poor performance of donors as they utterly failed in promoting Africa's sustained economic growth and fighting poverty.

President Paul Kagame of Rwanda was so inspired by the book that he called in Ms Moyo's help to wean Rwanda off its aid addiction. European Ministers for Development Aid are frantically reading the book; some even have invited Ms. Moyo to lecture. In Lusaka, the book is *the talk of the town* amongst the aid community.

Is her harsh judgment on the donors correct, let alone fair? This is the question I will deal with. But firstly, I will summarize *Dead Aid's* contents. The book consists of two parts. The first part is about the 'World of Aid', and the second is entitled 'A World without Aid'. At the end of part one she rightly says that development aid critics before her, such as William Easterly and Paul Collier, did not really provide alternatives for failing aid. Ms. Moyo *does* offer an alternative route to development which I will deal with below.

How did Africa fare during the past half century, having received more than one trillion of aid dollars. Ms. Moyo takes the reader through Africa's development since Independence. African policy makers followed successive mainstream development philosophies. Firstly, there was the state-led development philosophy. However, mismanagement, inefficiencies and falling export prices prompted many African governments to borrow (easy accessible) capital, to the extent that in the early 1980's quite a few of them were in fact bankrupt. This triggered structural adjustment, financed mainly by the IMF and World Bank. Many African countries had to restore order in their macro-economic and monetary policies as well as had to liberalise trade. At the turn of the Century, it was felt that impoverished and debt ridden African counties would never be able to develop if they were not relieved of their debts. After all, paying off debt depletes a country's financial resources which otherwise could have been invested in health, education and trade promotion. Hence, the enormous debt forgiveness wave, promoted by an odd combination of people such as Gordon Brown, Bono and the Pope!

Despite all the efforts, Africa's real per capita income today is lower than in the 1970's. While the number of the world's population and proportion of the world's people in extreme poverty fell after 1980, the number of Africans living in poverty nearly doubled.

Ms. Moyo concludes that it is impossible to draw on Africa's aid-led development experience and argue that aid has worked. Why is that, one may wonder? Because even when aid has not been stolen, it has been utterly unproductive. Donors failed to constrain corruption and bad government, Moyo says. These statements are typical for her dealing with the donors: she puts the blame for Africa's failure to grow squarely in their court. Ms. Moyo admits that Africa's failure to generate long-term growth must be a confluence of factors: geographical, historical, cultural, tribal and institutional. Apart from the fact that this is rather an *open door* statement, she does not elaborate it at all. Instead, she puts the spotlight on the donors' role once again: 'While each of these factors may be part of the explanation in differing degrees ... African countries have one thing in common-they all depend on aid'. I would like to add that, unfortunately, they have also a few other explanatory aspects in common, as Ms. Moyo herself so well characterized in her description of Dongo, a fictious African country, littered with man-made disincentives: widespread corruption, a maze of bureaucracy, a highly circumscribed regulatory and legal environment, and needless streams of red tape.

Ms. Moyo's analysis of the donors` role can at best be described as polemic. That is a pity, because she could have applied her sharp analytical skills with more depth and fairness in analysing their role. True, she admits that it was not donors' only role to help Africa grow; a lot of aid went to social development and humanitarian relief (often to help clean up the mess caused by man-made disasters), and to fight killer diseases such as malaria, TB and, more recently, HIV and AIDS. Yet, her main thesis is that aid props up corrupt governments who interfere with the Rule of Law and block the establishment of transparent institutions which hinder both domestic and foreign investment. Fewer investments reduce economic growth, which leads to fewer job opportunities and increasing poverty. In response to growing poverty, donors give more aid, which continues the downward spiral of poverty. But, are the donors the sole culprits? Donors are there to help countries develop, but if their leaders are not willing to do so, there is very little donors can do. What they then do is to try to prevent the situation from getting worse. I admit though that donors are sometimes persistent in supporting incompetent and/or corrupt governments.

Now, let us move to the second part 'A World Without Aid`. The solutions Ms. Moyo presents are in the domain of trade and development financing, with the exception of aid finance, of course. African countries should issue bonds in the commercial market place. Gabon has done so, and so has Ghana. Why are bonds a much better means to finance development than aid? Because the bond issuing country has to get a rating of its credit worthiness. However, to achieve this the country has to put order in vital financial and governance aspects. Secondly, evidence shows that the returns on bonds of emerging markets are much higher than on home bonds. Generating finance from bonds is more expensive than, say, a soft loan from the World Bank. But the author says that the fine print of these concessional loans proves to be costly, as the status-quo of aid dependency guarantees reputational damage. Ever present corruption and the negative stigma also form part of hidden costs. How much better, she says, if a country pays the higher financial rate, and gets quality investment and an improved standing in the world!

One crucial assumption is that African countries do indeed get an acceptable rating. The second one is that international finance would be available. When Ms. Moyo wrote the book, the credit crunch had not yet unfolded in all its devastating consequences. I fear that African countries will now have a very hard time to attract any foreign commercial financing. Moreover, Ms. Moyo admits that African countries have not improved their credit ratings over the past few years. Of the 35-odd African countries that had issued bonds in the international capital market around the mid-1990s, virtually all of them defaulted. In the subsequent thirty years, none of them have returned.

Moyo has, rightly, an open eye for the economic potential of Africa's poor. That potential should be unleashed through micro-credit, based on the Grameen Bank model; involving joint liability of small groups who together take loans and at the same time are encouraged to save. Then, there are remittances from Africans living overseas who send US$ 17 billion each year back home, much more than the amount of annual aid given. Invest those remittances productively, is what Ms. Moyo advocates, and introduce Diaspora bonds. Lastly, there are home-grown savings as an important source of investment and growth. This is still untapped as many African financial markets are inefficient: borrowers cannot borrow and lenders do not lend, despite the billions of dollars floating about, notes Moyo.

The fictious African country Dongo, Moyo concludes, should abandon the obsession with aid. It should plan for only 5 per cent of aid to finance its development; the rest is to come from bonds, trade, foreign direct investment, remittances and savings. The time to do so is more than ripe, now that Africa registers relatively high growth figures. Yet, governance has to be improved, because if money from the bond market is ill-spent or embezzled, surely no fresh money will be provided. Moyo writes: '.... in a world of good governance, which will naturally emerge in the absence of the glut of aid, the cost (risk) of doing business in Africa will be lower'.

Africa should turn to China for its future investments and development, says Moyo, not only because of its readiness to invest in health care and agriculture, but also because of China's commitment to foreign direct investment. She notes that China's African role is more sophisticated than any other country's at any time in the post-war period. Apparently, Ms. Moyo is fond of China's involvement in Africa, probably inspired by the notion that China will be a superpower before long, and because of its business-like attitude towards Africa. Hopefully, she will also watch China's protectionist policies regarding cotton for example, and its involvement in Africa from a governance point of view, which she underplayed.

The second part of the book is much more critical of the performance of African governments. The author notes that economic growth won't accelerate unless African policymakers remember that there are other developing regions where it is much easier to generate attractive returns with less hassle. This is probably not accidental as their leadership just cares more, Moyo states!

Dead Aid provides a road map to wean African countries off aid. With any addiction, that will not be easy. Ms. Moyo is not the first one to propose measures to get growth going. Does Ms. Moyo provide the solutions which will work? I am afraid not. Although her proposals would take away the negative effects of aid, she does not take into consideration the Dongo character of many African countries. Maybe this is because she is not living in one of them to experience the tremendous brakes put on any development by inefficient and corrupt governments and the very low quality of their education, as well as the sorry state of their infrastructure.

Maybe she is too optimistic about the effects of her development financing proposals. To tell you the truth, I'm not. I don't think that even a healthy financing basis of countries like Gabon and Ghana will propel development. The typical African country's institutions and accountability mechanisms are simply not good enough. Much more, including a lot of *patience* is required. Ms. Moyo rightly states that this 'much more' involves dramatically improving governance. Well, it is precisely the promotion of good governance which donors are supporting. There is nothing wrong in donors doing so, provided they act tough on non-compliance, and that has -I admit- not yet always been the case.

(2009)

The Return of History and the End of Dreams by Robert Kagan

The last decade of the twentieth century was an exciting one. The Berlin Wall fell, the Soviet Union imploded and the Cold War came to an end. We also witnessed an unprecedented expansion of the world's economy, propelled by China and India's enormous economic growth. But it was also the decade of growing resentment of Western especially American- domination, which found its strongest expression in Islamist fundamentalism, the attack of 11 September 2001 and the deepening political crisis in the Middle East. And since the beginning of this century, more countries developed nuclear weapons. The scramble for oil, gas and other natural resources became fiercer. Climate change and its possible consequences became more and more a concern.

It was also an exciting decade because the East-West divide became obsolete and new paradigms emerged. And it is about these paradigms that this review is about. In fact, the idea for it was inspired by the recent death of Harvard veteran Samuel Huntington, who published in 1997 *The Clash of Civilisations?* in which he presented a much darker view than another ground breaking book, which preceded Huntington's. The title of that book is *The End of History and the Last Man* written by Francis Fukuyama.

Fukuyama's book is *up-beat*; he concluded that the communist system had proven not to work. He argued that liberal democracy as a system of government had emerged throughout the world, as it had at the time conquered fascism and -most recently- communism. By the way, Fukuyama was not the only one to radiate an optimistic and self-assured mood: development thinkers believed that the *Washington Consensus* would bring about stability and growth in poor countries. Moreover, the 'peace dividend' resulting from less defence spending (after all, the Cold War was over!) could be used to provide more health and education services for the poor. I vividly remember that we were at the time indeed seriously discussing how best this peace dividend could be spent through increased aid for poor countries.

Huntington's views are gloomy. He did not subscribe to Fukuyama's triumphalistic ideas. Instead, he maintained that the old ideological

94

divisions of the Cold War would be replaced by even older cultural divisions. He said that the world was -and still is- very much divided between different civilisations. And far from overcoming the divide, Huntington foresaw these different cultures clashing into conflict.

Huntington also maintained that the Western civilisation was in relative decline. He said that: 'the future would be forged in the mosques of Tehran and the Planning Commission in Beijing, rather than in the cafés of Harvard Square'. Needless to say that he was very much opposed to the American neoconservative policy of invading Iraq in the spirit of the 'war against terror', which former President Bush declared after the 11 September 2001 onslaught on the USA. After the war would be won, democracy was to be promoted in Iraq, and throughout the Islamic world, it was thought.

Huntington first published his views in an article in 1993 in Harvard's monthly magazine *Foreign Affairs*. The reactions were so overwhelming, that it was translated in 26 languages and expanded into his 1997 best seller.

When we look back at what happened since 1997, Huntington predicted much better what really happened than Fukuyama and others. He came as close as anybody to predicting 9/11 and the war on terror. He also predicted America's frustrating attempts to introduce democracy in Iraq, by pointing out that democracy is the product of very specific cultural processes, and can't be smoothly introduced in such an ethnically and religiously divided country as Iraq.

Critics of Huntington's views point to the fact that he applied a very broad view, by not acknowledging that most bloody clashes took place *within* civilisations. A simple referral to Europe's bloody twentieth century is enough to underscore this point. He also downplayed the extent to which the American model attracts people the world over. A critic gave the following example: the Chinese and Indian business elite are much more interested in Silicon Valley than in their Confucian and Hindu past.

Huntington's vision was perceived in the Islamic world as specifically applying to them. Yet, most thinkers in the Arab world do not agree with Huntington's ideas. They considered them polemic and not based on a proper analysis. Moreover, they point to the fact that there is not one Islam; there are many varieties. Nonetheless, it is quite remarkable that Osama bin Laden belongs to the very few in the Islamic world who agrees with Huntington. His ideas can, after all, be seen as a *self fulfilling prophecy*, in the sense that after having been presented, they can be recognized in the 9/11 terrorist attack and the subsequent invasion in Iraq.

The world moved on since, and so did the ideas about grand designs. A very interesting proponent of a fresh worldview is Robert Kagan, who recently published a nice little book: *The Return of History and the End of Dreams*. What Kagan suggests is that the world has done away with the supremacy of liberal democracy. Kagan distances himself from Huntington's views, although not entirely. He analyses the world from a perspective of nationalist ambitions: the passions and the competition among nations that have shaped, and continue to shape history. True, the United States remains the sole superpower. But international competition among great powers has returned, with Russia, China, Europe, Japan, India and Iran vying for regional predominance. The old competition between liberalism and autocracy has re-emerged, with the world's great powers increasingly lining up according to the nature of their regimes. And an even older struggle has erupted between radical Islamists and the modern secular cultures and powers that, the Islamists believe, have dominated and polluted their Islamic world. These three struggles put together, promise little of Fukuyama's converging world; no, Kagan projects an age of divergence.

The attractiveness of Kagan's views is that they coincide with what is happening in the world today. The intriguing question, of course, is: how will it work out? Are we heading towards a (nuclear) World War? Will China eclipse the USA as the superpower, and what about Russia, with its enormous oil, gas and the natural resources reserves?

After the collapse of the Soviet Union in 1991, there was a temporary void in international relations: Russia was weakened, China had just started its phenomenal economic growth, India had not yet taken off, and Europe was rejecting power politics. At that time, Kagan concludes that the world was not witnessing a collective transformation into liberal democracies à la Fukuyama, but merely a pause in the age old competition of nations and peoples. In the course of the last decade of the twentieth century, one by one, rising powers entered the world stage: first China, then India, later followed by Russia and Brazil, promoted by their economic growth and increase in military might.

But well before this happened, Kagan also noted the global shift toward democracy of those nations who favoured the liberal democratic idea. That shift already began with the triumph of the democratic powers over fascism and -later- over communism in the Cold War. But those victories were not inevitable, warns Kagan, as today the re-emergence of the great autocratic powers, along the reactionary forces of Islamic radicalism, may well threaten that order.

Kagan concludes by saying that the United States, together with the rest of the democratic world, shares the responsibility to help solve global problems. The future international order will be shaped by those who have the power and collective will to shape it. The big question is whether the world's democracies will be able and willing again to rise to that challenge.

(2009)

The British Industrial Revolution in Global Perspective
by Robert Allen

Why should I bother to write about the Industrial Revolution which took place two hundred years ago? This seems a valid question, yet it was the economic revolution which catapulted many of the world's economies into a path of sustained growth. Its importance is also captured by what Karl Marx said: 'The industrially more developed country presents to the less developed country a picture of the latter's future'. After all, it is valuable to find out what factors brought the Industrial Revolution about.

Before 1800 economic growth was negligible; the economies of the world hovered around an equilibrium which was dictated by what agriculture could provide to the growing population. As soon as the population grew faster than agricultural output, famines occurred and the balance was restored. The Industrial Revolution changed all this dramatically. The other day I came across a book entitled: *The British Industrial Revolution in Global Perspective*, by the economic historian Robert Allen. He explains why the Industrial Revolution started in Britain and not in any other country.

Allen goes beyond the standard explanation that it was technological advances which triggered the Industrial Revolution. True, the steam engine, the cotton spinning machinery and the manufacture of iron with coal and coke (instead of charcoal) explain industrial expansion and further innovation. However, Allen points out that there were more factors, which -together- explain why Britain underwent the Industrial Revolution.

Now, what were these factors? Allen notes that Britain's wages were remarkably high in the 17th century, while energy was very cheap as there was a lot of coal available in Britain. The Industrial Revolution was invented in Britain *because it paid to invent it there*. Allen demonstrated that the British reacted to the economic incentives available to them; it paid to develop and apply technological inventions which replaced expensive labour and simultaneously boosted productivity.

But this was not all. Another factor was that Britain had developed

98

capitalistic institutions before the onset of the Industrial Revolution: Parliamentary democracy was established after the Glorious Revolution. The same applied to the securing of property rights.

The Scientific Revolution preceded the Industrial one. It started in Italy with Galileo and ended in England with Newton. The discoveries of 17th century physics were necessary conditions for the invention of the steam engine. But again, they were not sufficient to explain that the Industrial Revolution happened in England, as many of the scientific discoveries were done on the European continent. Nonetheless, the steam engine was invented in Britain. So, why was that? Well, argues Allen, turning scientific knowledge into working technology was an expensive undertaking. This proved to be worth its while only in England at the time, where the large coal industry created on the one hand a high *demand* for the drainage of the mines (by steam engines) and on the other an unlimited *supply* of virtually free fuel. Without Britain's unusual (high) wage and price structure, the research and development would not have been profitable.

Cultural evolution is another factor which was brought forward by historians in explaining the Industrial Revolution. Max Weber was a formidable proponent of the role of culture. He said that the Reformation led to modern Western rationality. It created the great divergence between the West and the Rest.

Allen proposes that three other aspects of cultural evolution happened with firm roots in the economic changes that took place even before the Industrial Revolution. They are (i) the spread of literacy and numeracy, (ii) the emergence of consumerism as a motive for wok, and (iii) the postponement of marriages when it was economically inconvenient. This new culture and the economy evolved together, each promoting the other. Cities, rural industry and commerce required skills that agriculture had not demanded. The invention of printing sharply reduced the price of books, leading to much more reading for useful knowledge, and for pleasure by the way. Literacy increased in England from 6 % in 1500 to 53 % in 1800. Knowledge of arithmetic and geometry was important to keep accounts and navigate merchant ships. The much greater level of human capital in the 18th century than in the Middle Ages is an important reason why the Industrial

Revolution didn't happen earlier. As for consumerism and hard work, new consumer goods were introduced in the British market: books, clocks and imported goods such as tea, spices and sugar, which all whetted consumers' appetite. And in order to buy them, money had to be earned through hard work. As for late marriages, these started to appear in Northwest Europe and not in any other part of the world. The relatively high wage rate economies in NW Europe triggered a strong demand for labour. This meant that young people -and young women in particular- could support themselves apart from their parents and control their lives and marriages. Women put off marriage until it suited hem.

As mentioned, central in Allen's explanation is the combination of high wages and cheap energy (coal). This made it possible for businesses to pay high wages and still remain competitive. Moreover, high wages and cheap energy made it profitable to invent technologies that substituted capital and energy for expensive labour. In other words, Britain's unique wage and price structure created the *demand* for the *supply* of technologies which brought production costs down.

But why were the wages so high? One has to go back in history to understand the upward trend. In the 17th and 18th century intercontinental trade expanded. The great gainers were the English and the Dutch who created large empires that fuelled their manufacture and commerce. Around 1500 most Europeans still lived in backward economies. This is indicated by the fraction of the population engaged in agriculture: roughly 75 %. This fraction dropped in England to 35 % by 1800; the biggest decline in Europe. An agricultural revolution, resulting in more agricultural output and less labour input, was part of the transformation of the English economy. This drop was matched by an increase in the urban population. Quite a bit of the urban growth was due to the growth of manufacturing and -in particular-commerce. Between 1500 and 1700 London's population grew ten-fold. The rapid rise in commerce and trade fuelled the standard of living and purchasing power of the British.

Allen concludes by saying that the Industrial Revolution was the result of a long process of social and economic evolution running back to the Middle Ages. The origin of the Industrial Revolution is the Black Death. Due to the bubonic plague many people died, triggering a high wage economy. England also started to produce better woollen products than their Italian competitors and their exports, through London, expanded fast. The growth of urban centres formed an impetus for advances in agricultural productivity. The early modern economy was underpinned by favourable institutional and cultural developments. The rise of a scientific attitude inclined more and more people to look for practical solutions to life's challenges. New products, many obtained from abroad (cotton, tea, spices, tobacco, etc.) enlarged the aspiration to consume and increased the incentive to earn high incomes. Political institutions, favourable to capitalist development, as well as the growth of literacy, numeracy and of hard work followed from the expansion of international commerce and the rapid growth of cities. But the upshot of the commercial expansion was the unique wage and price structure that Britain enjoyed in the 18th century. This led directly to the Industrial Revolution by giving firms strong incentives to invent technologies that substituted capital and coal for labour.

Allen's fascinating explanation tells us that the quest for growth cannot be found in a single factor, such as *getting the institutions right*. Growth and development are the result of the interplay between quite a few factors, some of which have to do with available resources, others with geographical location, but the most important -I find- is what the people, their leaders, and societies at large do (or not do!) with the opportunities provided to them.

(2010)

CRISES

Thought for Food; the International Food Crisis

A crisis never comes alone. The present international financial crisis was preceded by the energy crisis, and now we witness the devastating effects of the food crisis. None of them is expected to go away soon. This article is about the international food crisis; its causes, the effects it has on the one billion poor of this world, and what can be done about it.

Food is the most basic consumer commodity. For the poor it is the single most important expense. Unaffordable food triggers unrest, riots, bloodshed and it undermines political stability. In Haiti, the prime minister was forced to resign after fierce protests in which 5 protesters died; 24 people were killed in riots in Cameroon; in Senegal protests were fierce. President Mubarak of Egypt had to order the army to start baking bread; the Philippines made hoarding rice punishable. In Bangladesh thousands of garment workers went on strike for higher pay to cope with soaring food prices. In Argentina the Minister of Agriculture had to resign after farmers fiercely protested against his intention to increase the export tax on agricultural produce.

The immediate cause of the protests is the steep rise in food prices. Last year, wheat prices rose 77 % and rice 16 %. Worse, this year the speed of the price hike has accelerated. Since January, rice prices have soared 141 %, and the price of one variety of wheat shot up 25 % in one day! What does this mean for the poor? For those on $2 budget per day, it means no more meat, and taking the children out of school. For those living of $1 a day, it means cutting out meat and vegetables, and eating only cereals. And for the real destitute (half a dollar a day) it means total disaster. Food inflation may put at least 100 million people into poverty, reckons Robert Zoellick, the World Bank's President, wiping out all the gains the poorest billion have made during almost a decade of economic growth. During the recent Spring Meeting of the IMF and World Bank in Washington DC, Zoellick proposed a *New Deal* to address the crisis. The Bank's intention is to financially help the poor who are hardest hit by the crisis. This helps keeping them alive, prevent demand from plummeting and helps to ensure that small food sellers would not go out of business.

104

The steep rise in food prices mainly reflects changes in demand and not so much problems of supply, such as harvest failures. These changes in demand include the increased purchasing power of people in China and India, who now can afford to eat more grain and meat. Another demand factor is the lucrative conversion of agricultural produce into bio fuel. This year the share of maize crop going into ethanol in the USA has risen and the European Union is implementing its own bio fuel targets. These shifts have not (yet) been matched by increase in production. The good news is that farmers will react and food supplies will increase to once again match demand, most probably on a higher price level than in the past.

In the past we had localised food crises; Ethiopia, Bangladesh, and the Sahel countries come to mind. Now, the present crisis is affecting many -especially- poor countries and all at the same time. What can -and should- be done in the short term is (i) to prop up the budget of the World Food Programme with the requested $700 million, (ii) finance well targeted social protection programmes, and (iii) the introduction of favourable trade policies. But the question remains what should be done in the medium term; how can more food be produced? If the extra food comes from the traditional suppliers such as the USA, Europe and Argentina, the world will remain dependent on them. US farmers are already responding in that their winter wheat planting is up by 4 % and the spring sown area is likely to rise even more. The Food and Agriculture Organisation predicts that Europe's wheat harvest will rise 13 % this year. Russia is also expanding its agricultural production.

Spreading risk is always good, that also goes for food production. Developing countries have 450 million smallholders, who each farm only a few acres. If development policies, and development aid, be more geared to them it would have 3 advantages: (i) poverty of the smallholders will be reduced, (ii) it might help the environment as the smallholders manage a very large share of the world's water and vegetation cover; hence, raising their productivity on the land they occupy would be environmentally friendlier than cutting down the rainforest to make way for more arable land, and (iii) it is efficient, but this needs a bit of explanation. It is easier to raise yields in Africa from 2 tonnes to 4 tonnes per hectare for example than it would be to raise 8 to 10 tonnes in Europe, because the *law of diminishing returns* is applicable to Europe but not yet to Africa's smallholders. Fine, this smallholder would say, but what about the rising price of fertilisers? That is a factor to reckon with as anecdotal evidence has it that smallholders are not responding enough yet to the higher prices they can fetch for their crops. At any event, producing more food crops takes time; after all, one can not sow and harvest the next day; the increase in sales price will thus result in a positive supply response later. Moreover, smallholders typically have limited areas of fallow land which could be planted. And the area suitable for rice farming is getting smaller worldwide, as a result of urbanisation. Hence, more food production from the large army of smallholders will have to primarily come from higher yields.

Research to improve productivity and to develop more high yielding seed varieties and better fertilisers also takes time. Sadly, public spending in developing countries on farming and research fell by half between 1980 and 2004. The response of smallholders may also be less than expected because they have more difficulties to get credit than commercial farmers, and they are no match for big traders and supermarkets who require uniform high quality and large quantities. It is expected, however, that if prices keep on being high, the smallholders may in the medium term be able to respond and benefit.

Technological improvements will also help. The International Rice Research Institute in the Philippines expects that its work on higher yielding rice seeds may increase yields by one or two tonnes per hectare. A more controversial productivity booster is the genetically modified organisms (to which European countries are still hostile), which could boost yields 50 % or more.

Zambia's Central Bank President rightly urged Zambia's farmers to increase food production, not only to consolidate Zambia's food security, to help dampen the upward push of food prices, but also to help mitigate the imminent food shortages worldwide, while benefiting from attractive prices. Dr. Fundanga said that Zambia has got the land and natural resources for increased crop production. Zambia can produce more rice and wheat. Obviously, this requires an urgent effort in satisfying increasing energy needs. And feeder roads will have to be constructed, and the existing road network requires dramatic improvement and proper maintenance.

Credit availability and the rising costs of inputs form challenges but these can be overcome with the right Government help.

Zambia can thus benefit from favourable food prices through the rapid expansion of its agricultural sector which will also result in more export earnings, in dampening the price for local food stuffs and it can contribute to the world's supply of agricultural produce. In other words: Zambia, the challenge is yours!

(2008)

Can the International Food Crisis be Countered?

All news networks report daily about protests against sky rocketing food prices. Understandably, most of the protests are staged in poor countries because the pain is felt hardest there. The World Bank says that the gains made during the past decade in fighting poverty could be partly reversed as 100 million people may again be plunged in absolute poverty, precisely because of the higher prices they have to pay for their food.

Now, what factors have caused the sudden rise in the price of wheat, maize, rice and other staple foods? Will the world's demand for food permanently outstrip supply, and what can be done about it? When looking for answers, one is sometimes tempted to side with the new Malthusians, as I would call them, and other times with their opponents: the Positivists. There are no unequivocal answers to be given to the questions I just presented. This is, I believe, caused by the fact that conflicting data are presented in the debate, and crises -like the present one- also bring out emotional reactions.

Let me deal first with the *new Malthusians* whose opinions are inspired by the thinking of Thomas Robert Malthus (1776 - 1834). Malthus, who was a pastor before becoming professor of economics in Cambridge, maintained that during his lifetime the population in England grew exponentially, while the food production only grew in a linear fashion. Malthus concluded that if something was not done about birth control, a huge famine would result, after which the equilibrium would be restored. Malthus had many followers, but we know now that his projections were wrong: the birth rate went down, and food production increased much more than he thought.
Yet, it is not surprising that Malthusian thoughts crop up again, now that we are faced with steep price rises for food, reflective of food supply falling short of growing demand. The new Malthusians fear that a structural food shortage is looming at the horizon.

However, *the Positivists* contest that the world is structurally running out of food. Louise Fresco, former assistant Director General of the Food and Agriculture Organisation (FAO), says that there is enough agricultural potential in the world to even feed the 9 billion people the world will have by 2050, provided the productivity of the 450 million small-holder farmers is increased, amongst others through technological progress, and that harvests are not eaten up by rats or be spoiled during transport or bad storage.

Now let us look a bit more at the pattern of food prices. Historically speaking, food prices have hardly increased since World War II; they were on their lowest level in 2000. It is not so surprising that the prices have risen since. The price of one tonne of wheat increased from $167 in January 2006 to $481 two years later. The price of rice more than tripled over the past two years: from $300 to USD 1,000 per tonne. Overall, food prices doubled during the past five years, *partly* caused by increased demand, especially from China and India. There the eating habits changed in favour of more meat, and you need three times as much agricultural land to produce meat compared to what you need for a vegetarian diet. But other factors are at play as well, such as the sudden and sharp increase in the price of oil, fertilisers and phosphates. Bad harvests partly caused by the influence of climate change, in Australia, India, Southern Europe, the USA, and- tragically- in Burma, added to the upward pressure. At the same time agricultural land in Europe was taken out of production. The increase of food prices triggered export bans in many food exporting countries, such as Argentina, Cambodia, India and Vietnam.

Another reason, one often hears, is the production of bio-fuel, triggered by the high oil price. This is a good example of the messiness of the debate. In fact only 2 % of the world´s agricultural area is now devoted to bio-fuel. Moreover, Brazil, for example, is already producing ethanol from sugar cane for decades. There is more controversy on bio-fuels. The American Secretary of Agriculture, Ed Schafer, maintains that bio-fuel production is responsible for only 2 - 3 % of the increase in world food prices. However, the International Food Policy Research Institute says the increase is 30 %. The dwindling world stocks of wheat (at the moment at their lowest levels in decades) definitely have an upward price influence, because they can not properly function as a buffer to counter price increases. The agricultural sector has been neglected in many developing countries: only 0.5 % of GDP is invested in agriculture in Sub-Saharan Africa, compared to 2 % in developed countries.

As for perverse elements, speculators further contribute to the steep increase in prices. And institutional investors are looking for greener pastures after the credit crunch; they massively invest in wheat, maize, rice, and the like. In 2006 world-wide investment in raw materials (including food) was USD 70 billion; two months ago the amount had risen to USD 235 billion! FAO´s and OECD´s most recent *Agricultural Outlook* report predicts that the food prices will drop slightly, after which they will stabilise at a higher average level than in the past. Price volatility will remain fairly high because of the entry of large non-food investors in the market.

What does the link between trade, food prices and poverty reduction tell us? It is difficult to accept that food social safety nets were hardly discussed during the recent Food Summit held in Rome. The reason is probably that the participating countries had varying interests. This is the more strange now that some international financial institutions have indicated their readiness to help poor African countries in (co)financing social safety nets and the expansion of the domestic agricultural sector.

A recent World Bank study concluded that net food buyers tend to be richer than net sellers. So, high food prices, on average, transfer income from richer to poorer households. And prices are not the only way in which poverty is affected. Higher farm income boosts demand for rural labour, increasing wages for landless peasants and others who buy rather than grow their food. This income effect can outweigh the initial price hike, studies tell us. Moreover, the farm sector itself can grow as well. Decades of underinvestment in agriculture have left many poor countries reliant on imports, and over time that can change. All told, if there would be free trade in food stuffs this would, on balance, help reduce poverty in the majority of poor countries.

What Louise Fresco said about increasing productivity of small-holder farmers, was echoed by the Zambian National Farmers Union's (ZNFU) past Chairman, Guy Robinson. He said during the recently held *Euro Money* seminar in Lusaka, that out of ZNFU`s 600,000 members 400,000 are small farmers. And their production can go up from 1.2 tonnes per hectare to 5 tonnes, if they would have proper access to markets and would have land titles giving them access to credit. As for the large farmers, Robinson lamented about the lack of long-term credit available to them, about Zambia's ill-managed fertiliser subsidy scheme, and about the bad quality of feeder roads. He suggested government to lower the tariffs on gasoline and diesel. Hence, productivity can be greatly improved if more land would be under title deeds and if there would be better access to credit. And that would be to everybody's benefit: the farmer would earn more because he produces more. Triggered by it, more landless labourers will be employed which raises their income, and the government would receive more tax income. The incentive to swiftly act is already there: much better prices for agricultural and dairy products! So, Zambia's economic boom can be broadened if and when government, and other actors such as banks, take away the obstacles to fully grasp its agricultural potential.

(2008)

From One Crisis to the Other

A friend of mine just came back from New York where he spent the Christmas holidays. Since he is a devout reader, the first thing he did was to enter one of Barnes & Nobles bookstores to look what books they had as special offers. All of them dealt with the international financial crisis: Books on end explaining where the crisis came from, what happened, how bad it is and what should have been done about it. One classic which my friend missed amongst all the books on the crisis was John Kenneth Galbraith's *The Great Crash 1929*. He asked the bookseller why Galbraith's acclaimed book was not on display. He exclaimed: 'Jesus, sold out again!' The Americans apparently want to know what happened in 1929 to -hopefully- learn from it.

John Kenneth Galbraith (1908-2006) was probably the most influential economist during the 1950s and 1960s. His most popular work is *The Affluent Society* which he published in 1958, and which was on the best sellers list for 30 weeks on end. His writing of *The Great Crash 1929* came about when he got stuck in writing *The Affluent Society*. He was lucky enough that his neighbour was the political historian Arthur Schlesinger Jr. who at the time was working on a book about President Roosevelt. Schlesinger suggested Galbraith: 'Why not write the definitive book on the Crash; that would help me greatly in putting Roosevelt's *New Deal* in perspective'. And so Galbraith did during the beautiful summer of 1954. Galbraith later said that he never enjoyed writing a book more than the Great Crash! I happened to have a copy which I had never read, so I used the Christmas holidays to have a go at it. I enjoyed reading it, despite the dismal subject of the Wall Street crash and the ensuing 10 years world-wide economic depression. Before dealing with what Galbraith had to say about the Great Crash, I like to tell you a bit more about Galbraith.

The Canadian John Kenneth Galbraith had the great gift of writing in a lucid and sometimes tongue in-cheekish way, making his many readers believe that economics is a jolly subject and not a *dismal science*. It must have been quite a disappointment for Galbraith not to have been awarded the Nobel Prize for Economics. That may have been because he was more a populariser of economics than a contributor of new insights to the body of knowledge. After all, Galbraith felt that economics is not a real science; it is a tool to interpret present day circumstances. Moreover, by the time the first Nobel Prize for Economics was awarded in the early 1970s, Galbraith's fame was fading because he was a Keynesian, and Keynesian economics had been eclipsed by Milton Friedman's neo-classical economics. Yet, typical for Galbraith, when addressing a large audience (I was amongst the crowd) in Amsterdam in the early 1990s, he started his lecture by saying: 'I am the greatest living economist; as I measure 1 meter and 95 centimetres and there is not a taller economist around!'

Now, back to the subject matter. *The Great Crash* is a lucid story about the prelude to the dramatic drop in share prices on Wall Street, and about that fateful month of October 1929. The book also deals with the question why it took a decade to recover from the Depression. Like other economic bubbles, such as the crazy speculation trade in tulip bulbs in 17th century Holland, the Great Crash was preceded by the lunatic Florida land speculation in the 1920s. By the way, the present financial crisis was triggered by the collapse of the housing bubble in the United States. As for the land speculation bubble, decision makers were indecisive; most wanted the bubble to continue as so many benefitted from it and feared the consequences of a sudden burst. As Galbraith put it: 'A bubble can be easily punctured. But to incise it with a needle so that it subsides gradually is a task of no small delicacy'. The mood in the United States at the end of the 1920s was, in Galbraith's words, a mass escape from reality. Every American had the right to become rich overnight, it was thought and quite a few did! There was a speculative craze, also funnelled by new investment models, such as Investment Trusts. The striking thing about the stock market speculation was not the massiveness of the participation; it was the way it became central to the American *culture*. Warnings of an imminent collapse were scarce; *The New York Times* being the exception, but it was obviously not listened too. Others, including respected economists such as Irving Fisher and also the Harvard Economic Society kept on saying that the economy was basically in good shape. After all, during the summer of 1929 alone, stocks had risen by 25 %. Needless to say that Wall Street became more and more detached from the real world of Main Street.

By the autumn of 1929 the US economy was already well into a recession. On top of that, home building had been ailing for several years and slumped further in 1929. And then, finally, came the Crash on Black Thursday 24 October 1929. Close to 13 million shares changed hands. Panic had stricken. But not to the extent that hundreds of stockbrokers and others having lost all their capital jumped out of the windows of Manhattan's skyscrapers. Galbraith even checked the suicide rate at the time. This appeared not to have been appreciably higher than in other periods. He noted, though, that at the time clerks in downtown hotels were said to be asking guests whether they wished the room for sleeping or jumping. True enough, a couple of notorious fraudulent financiers (the likes of present day Bernard Madoff, responsible for the $50 billion Pyramid Fund swindle) committed suicide.

The New York Stock Exchange was supposed to be a self regulating body. It was only in 1934 that the Security and Exchange Commission (SEC) was formed as the regulatory body; incidentally, the very same institution which failed to spot the recent enormous Madoff swindle.

That the Crash led to such a long lasting world-wide depression was caused by various factors. Galbraith says that one explaining factor was the optimistic and speculative mood, to the extent that stock prices were no longer reflective of the real value of companies whose shares were traded on Wall Street and not reflective of the already ongoing recession. New investments were sharply curtailed, which in turn promoted the downward spiral. Furthermore, the American income distribution at the end of the 1920's was very uneven. Resumed growth should have come from spending of the rich and/or fresh investments. Since the rich were hit hardest by the Crash, and there were no new investments, demand dropped further. The banking system was also weak; one bank after another collapsed. Additional important explanations can be found in the economic philosophies at the time. One was that government's budget should be balanced; whilst -as John Maynard Keynes later explained- in times of depression economic stimulus should come from deficit financing by government. Incidentally, President Obama has understood this crucial message very well! Even before his inauguration on 20 January 2009, he already urged Congress to accept his huge stimulus plan, to prevent the American economy from sliding in a deep recession, comparable to the one of the 1930`s. Another hindering factor was the obsessive relationship between the dollar and the Gold Standard. Devaluation of the dollar (which could have boosted exports) was flatly ruled out, as it was thought that this would promote inflation, which was seen as a horror, as demonstrated by Germany's dramatic hyper inflation at the time, comparable to present day's Zimbabwe.

Keynesian economics has again taken centre stage in these times of crisis. And it is not a co-incidence that, once again, Galbraith is a best-seller author, be it a posthumous one.

(2009)

The International Economic Crisis

The world is facing the worst economic recession since 80 years. The world economy is declining steeply. Stock markets took a deep plunge, preceded by the housing market collapse in the USA and Great Britain. Millions lost their pension entitlements. Consumers curtailed spending. They now prefer to save. Quite a few banks went broke. The remaining ones try to get their balance sheets in order with the help of billions of dollars of government aid. Lending is heavily curtailed. This in turn limits investments, forcing companies to slash production. Millions lost their jobs, not only in the USA and Europe, but also in China. International trade has shrunk at the fastest rate since World War II, hitting export-oriented countries hard.

The Organisation for Economic Cooperation and Development (OECD) forecasts that the world economy will shrink by 2.7 % this year. It thinks that its (rich) member countries will see their output fall by more than 4 %. That would be by far the deepest synchronized downturn since 1929, the year of the Great Crash. The OECD also expects growth to stay well below its trend rate next year, widening the rich world's output gap - which is the distance between the economy's actual and potential performance - to an extraordinary 8.5 % of GDP. That would bring many countries close to deflation which, incidentally, prolonged the economic crisis of the 1930's. It was John Maynard Keynes who -at the time- pointed at this dangerous downward spiral, and proposed government promoted economic stimulus.

These stimulus packages are now applied by way of a world-wide synchronised macroeconomic response. During the recent G-20 meeting in London it was agreed to *triple* the financial firepower of the IMF, to -especially- help those emerging economies which don't have the means to re-ignite their economies. Short-term interest rates have been slashed. The impact of lower tax revenues and higher jobless payments will result in the rich world's jump in budget deficits by about six percentage points of GDP. During that same G-20 meeting, the participating countries vowed to fight protection, a threat looming over the world economy. After all, it is attractive for government leaders to save local jobs by banning (cheaper) imported goods and services.

The question is whether this economic counter offensive is enough to prevent the situation of the 1930's when the depression lasted almost ten years. No one really knows. The only thing we know is that the world economy has never looked as bad since the 1930's. However, recently small signs of improvement were reported. In the USA consumer spending is no longer in free fall and the housing market (where the trouble started) shows signs of stabilizing. In Britain mortgage lending may have hit the bottom. Consumers are a little less gloomy and manufacturing looks less depressing. Stock markets are picking up. These are only glimmers of hope. It may be that they peter out. It is too early to conclude that the world economy has turned the corner.

What does this economic gloom mean for poor countries? From the outset it must be put on record that they did not have a hand whatsoever in the collapse of the world economy. Yet, they pay a heavy price as the recession is now hitting the *bottom billion, i.e.* the poorest people in some 60 poor countries, most of them in Africa. The continent may not have been hit so hard as yet; however, the recession will certainly punch many African countries in the face later this year. The IMF has just cut its forecast for economic growth in Africa this year to 3.6 % from its original forecast 6.7 %. IMF's Managing Director, Strauss Kahn, told a conference in Tanzania that millions of Africans could be thrown back into poverty by the crisis.

The global meltdown affects poor countries in three ways. First, there is capital: private capital flows dry up for poor countries; credit is in short supply, hurting borrowers (especially micro-credit takers) in poor countries. According to the Institute of International Finance, net private capital flows to poor countries will plunge from almost $1 trillion in 2007 to $165 billion in 2009. African countries were able in 2007 to raise $6.5 billion in international bonds (thus having done what *Dambisa Moyo* proposed). But in 2008 they didn't manage to raise anything at all. This year the situation will not be any better. Also investments are called off. For instance, steel giant Arcelor-Mittal slashed an iron-ore project in Liberia. Malawi was hit by the deferral of a large uranium project which was supposed to contribute 10 % of the national income.

Foreign aid is an important source for the poor. The Overseas Development Institute calculates that aid flows may fall by $20 billion this year. As most aid goes to Africa, the African poor will feel the pain most. But this is not all. Commodity prices, such as the copper price, dropped. Imports from Sub-Saharan Africa dropped by 12 %. The African Development Bank says that African current accounts, which were in surplus by 3.8 % of GDP in 2007, will be 6 % in the red this year. Most African governments' budgets will leave no room for economic stimulus. Then, there are remittances. These amounted to $300 billion in 2008; more than the total amount of foreign aid for Africa, by the way. But remittances are now falling as many countries send guest workers back home.

As capital inflows and investments vanish, poor countries face a mounting debt. Tragically, all the problems follow a decade of growth which has lifted millions out of extreme poverty. Many of the poor may now slip below the extreme poverty line of $1.25 a day. World Bank's poverty expert, Martin Ravallion, estimates that 53 million people will fall below that line this year. The consequences of the world-wide economic crisis will be tragic. The World Bank estimates that between 200,000 and 400,000 *more* children will die every year between now and 2015. The sad conclusion is that progress towards a richer, more equitable world has been set back by years!

Now, what is the outlook for Zambia? Its main export product, copper, has dropped in price. Investments in copper mining and exploration have been dropped or postponed. 8,000 Layoffs have taken place and may continue. Tax revenues will be far less than anticipated. GDP will grow less than 5 % this year, while the original estimate was 7 %. The kwacha has depreciated, which may help boost other export products; who knows. Paradoxically, the economic downturn may not impact very much on Zambia's poor. Being insulated from the formal economy, the poor hardly benefitted from the past ten years of 5 % average annual economic growth. The downturn will be much more felt in urban areas, including on the Copperbelt where layoffs are already taking place. Those affected may return to rural areas, as it happened in earlier lean times.

The most damaging effect of the recession is on government's finances. Until recently, mining taxes contributed 1.4 % of GDP. The introduction of the new mining tax last year, was supposed to result in revenues of 4.6 % of GDP this year. This would have given government more income to spend on e.g. health and education and on targeted poverty alleviation programs. But the government issued tax concessions to the mines to save jobs there. As a result, the mining tax is now estimated to bring in only 0.5 % of GDP. However, the projections of foreign aid indicate that -for the moment- the amounts may not drop significantly. Should the economy worsen further, government may have to launch counter measures such as a stimulus package and social protection programs for which additional finances will have to be sought.

(2009)

Keynes and Again Keynes

Keynes is in fashion again, like he was 60 years ago. This is because his ideas about countering the Great Depression of the 1930s have been re-appreciated now that the world is facing the deepest recession since then. Now, who was Keynes, what were exactly his ideas and why was it that he was out of fashion for quite some time?

John Maynard Keynes (1883 - 1946) was a brilliant British economist who created a new economic theory to effectively deal with economic recessions. He presented this theory in 1936 in a book entitled *The General Theory of Employment, Interest and Money*. His proposals were immediately put to action, for example through President Roosevelt's New Deal, and greatly helped putting an end to the deep economic crisis of the 1930's. Keynesianism became the mainstream economic thinking until the early 1970s, when the world's richest economies entered into a situation of inflation and unemployment. Then the New Classical school of thought got the upper hand; but now it is again Keynes who is calling the shots!

A stale joke about economists is that when the economy does not reflect what the economic theory of the day prescribes, there is something wrong with the economy and not with the theory. As regards the present economic recession, the mainstream economic theories didn't predict it, let alone helped to prevent it. Hence, not only is the economy in crisis, the economic science as well. The trouble is that economics is not really a science, such as physics or chemistry. Time and again economics is overtaken by the facts, it adjusts accordingly and the adjustment becomes mainstream until developments in the real world prove mainstream thinking inadequate.

The conclusion one can draw from these changing paradigms is that no economic theory has so far been able to capture the developments of the real economy and that, depending on the state of the economies (i.e. steady growth or recession), economic theories and prescriptions (re)emerge subsequently. It is therefore not surprising that there is disagreement between economists. Robert Waldmann, economics professor at Rome

University, distinguishes between two types of economists: freshwater and saltwater economists both inspired by the New Classical school of thought.

The freshwater ones, trained at Chicago, consider general equilibrium models with well-functioning markets and symmetric information to be decent approximations to reality and eschew government intervention. Saltwater macroeconomics, while accepting the basic principles of the New Classical school, gives more room for policy *interference* than the mainstream New Classicals.

Freshwater economists assume rational expectations, i.e. everyone knows the future behaviour of the markets and they conceive the *economic agents as perfectly informed*, which -may I note- one doesn't come across often in real life. Saltwater macroeconomics, which is known as New Keynesianism, is basically everything else, while underscoring the fundamental importance of incomplete markets and of asymmetric information and of imperfect competition. Saltwater economists develop models which allow scope for policy intervention in the *short run*. This is contrary to the freshwater economists who deny these interventions, as they maintain that in a crisis situation market forces themselves will in the *long run* re-establish economic equilibrium. Thus the New Keynesians make use of the distinction between the long and the short run. In the short run they propose effective adjustment measures. They are necessary because demand has to be stimulated to pull the economy out of a crisis.

This seems such a simple reasoning; however, at the time the Classical School claimed that people wanted to save only in order to invest, so the savings accumulated would lead sooner or later to investments, and the economy would be in equilibrium again; there would not be a gap between them. Keynes's idea was quite revolutionary as he showed that there isn't always enough investment to make use of the savings. Keynes explained how this could have happened. In essence it comes down to the following: investments depend on *expectations* about future developments. Keynes said that savings would *not* automatically lead to investment, as a great deal of saving is a demand for cash and *not* a demand for investment goods. And the demand for cash increases the more uncertain the prospects for investment become, such as in a crisis situation. Hence, more is saved and less is spent, resulting in a dearth in demand. The Great Depression of the 1930's saw the dramatic collapse of demand resulting in mass unemployment.

In the 1970's Keynes's policies didn't have an answer to *stagflation* (simultaneous increase in inflation and unemployment) which was then the main problem. The New Classical economists did, inspired by Milton Friedman from the Chicago school of economists. He noted that there were increasing rigidities in the labour market (pushing the costs of labour up) leading to double digit inflation and unemployment, which at the time was partly compensated by unemployment payments by governments. Friedman's recipe was to promote private enterprise through lower taxes and less regulation. Friedman became the new prophet of the free market; his policy prescriptions being eagerly applied by then President Reagan and Prime Minister Thatcher. Just as Keynes succeeded politically because unemployment was the problem in the 1930's, Friedman succeeded politically because inflation was the main problem of the 1970's.

As a result of the present crisis the free market system -hailed as the solution to the problems of the Keynesian era - collapsed and Keynes's policies are not only re-appreciated but again widely applied. The present recession is, as investor George Soros noted: 'Generated by the system itself'.

The crisis started in the USA. Firstly, the housing boom collapsed as a result of the increase in the US interest rate and because mortgages had been issued to people who in fact could not afford them. Second, securitization worsened the problem. Securitization is the process of bundling up individual mortgages and then slicing them into different securities (to spread the risk)tailored to the requirement of the different investors, which are then sold on by the originating bank. When home owners started to default on their mortgages, the banks' investments had turned illiquid. Banks were finding it increasingly hard to raise fresh money from other banks. The credit freeze spread from the banks to their customers. The scene was set for a classic downward slide from banking failure to stock market failure and to decline in the real economy. Thirdly, bank regulation had fallen grossly short as it was assumed that the financial markets would regulate themselves. Former FED President Alan Greenspan admitted that the whole intellectual edifice on which the economy was built collapsed; it could not predict nor explain the economic meltdown, precisely because -as already noted- the majority of economists were of the view that markets are self-correcting. As a result, governments have returned to Keynes's main advice, i.e. to promote aggregate demand through financial injections into the ailing economy to bail out banks saddled with toxic assets, to help struggling firms, etc., in order to recover growth.

The Great Depression of the 1930s lasted almost 10 years. Thanks to Keynes's insights in addressing crises and thanks to the stimulus packages which were swiftly put in place by governments of the world's main affected economies, it now seems as if the worst part of the present recession is over.

(2010)